# Places In Time

A Kid's Historic Guide to the Changing Names and Places of the World

## A Brief Political and Geographic History of the

# Middle East

Where Are···· Persia, Babylon, and the Ottoman Empire

Mitchell Lane
PUBLISHERS

P.O. Box 196
Hockessin, Delaware 19707
Visit us on the web: www.mitchelllane.com
Comments? email us: mitchelllane@mitchelllane.com

## A Brief Political and Geographic History of the

# Middle East

Where Are . . . Persia, Babylon, and the Ottoman Empire

John Davenport

**Mitchell Lane**
**PUBLISHERS**

P.O. Box 196
Hockessin, Delaware 19707
Visit us on the web: www.mitchelllane.com
Comments? email us: mitchelllane@mitchelllane.com

Printing          1          2          3          4          5          6          7          8          9

**Library of Congress Cataloging-in-Publication Data**
Davenport, John, 1960–
    A brief political and geographic history of the Middle East ; where are Persia, Babylon, and the Ottoman Empire? / By John Davenport.
        p. cm. — (Places in time/a kid's historic guide to the changing names and places in the world)
    Includes bibliographical references and index.
    ISBN 978-1-58415-622-2 (library bound)
    1.  Middle East—History—Juvenile literature. I. Title.
DS62.D384 2007
956—dc22
                                                                                                     2007000795

PHOTO CREDITS: Maps by Jonathan Scott—pp. 6, 7, 8, 15, 18, 25, 28, 35, 38, 45, 48, 55, 58, 65, 68, 75, 78, 87, 90, 99; p. 10—Superstock; pp. 11, 12, 17, 23, 27, 34, 36, 37, 40, 44, 46, 57, 86, 89—JupiterImages; p. 13—Suzanne Held; p. 14—Giraudon/Art Resource; p. 16—Haydar Hatemi; p. 20—Gerry Lynch; p. 21—Desmond Harney/RHPL; p. 24—Louvre Museum, Paris; p. 30—Austen Henry Layard; p. 32—Zyworld; p. 42—Three Lions/Getty Images; p. 43—William Blake; p. 47—Trouce/Creative Commons; pp. 50, 51, 53, 62, 77—Hulton Archive/Getty Images; p. 54—Stock Montage/Getty Images; p. 56—Jean Fouquet; p. 60—Jamie Kondrchek; p. 64—Thomas Ihle/German Wikipedia; p. 66—Ginolerhino/Creative Commons; p. 70—Ghirlandajo/Derbent Fortress; p. 71—Library of Congress; p. 72—General Photographic Agency/Getty Images; p. 73—GFDL; p. 74—Time Life Pictures/Mansell/Getty Images; p. 76—Muriel Gottrop; p. 81—Muhannad Fata'h/Getty Images; p. 82—Ali Mansuri/Creative Commons; p. 85—China Photos/Getty Images; p. 88—Eugène Ferdinand Victor Delacroix/Musée du Louvre, Paris; p. 92—Tim Graham/Getty Images; p. 93—Steve Evans/Creative Commons; p. 95—Jean-Joseph Benjamin-Constant/Art Renewal Center Museum; p. 96—Nikolay Nikolaevich Karazin; p. 98—NASA; p. 100—nomo/Michael Hoefner/Creative Commons; p. 112—Jennifer Davenport.

PUBLISHER'S NOTE: This story is based on the author's extensive research, which he believes to be accurate. Documentation of such research is contained on page 106.

The internet sites referenced herein were active as of the publication date. Due to the fleeting nature of some web sites, we cannot guarantee they will all be active when you are reading this book.

To reflect current usage, we have chosen to use the secular era designations BCE ("before the common era") and CE ("of the common era") instead of the traditional designations BC ("before Christ") and AD (*anno Domini,* "in the year of the Lord").

PLB

# Places In Time

## Table of Contents

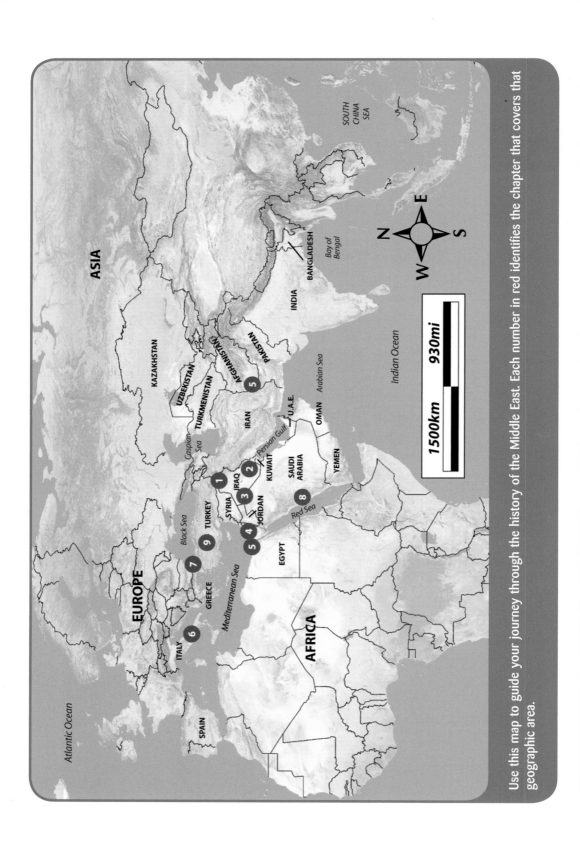

Use this map to guide your journey through the history of the Middle East. Each number in red identifies the chapter that covers that geographic area.

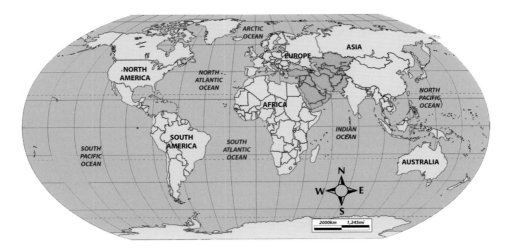

Persia, Bablyon, and the Ottoman Empire ··· Where Are...

## Introduction

Perhaps no place on earth is in the news more often than the Middle East. Most often the stories one reads in the newspapers or sees on the television have to do with some kind of trouble. Access to oil, the misuse of nuclear power, and terrorism dominate the conversation whenever broadcasters, politicians, or just average people gather to discuss a huge part of the globe that reaches from the Mediterranean Sea to the borders of India. But there is much more to the Middle East than that. Despite its problems and conflicts, the Middle East is a region rich in culture and history, a history that covers well-known places as well as those that have been long forgotten, the only traces of which lie in ruined cities and ancient artifacts.

This book surveys the history of the Middle East and explores some of the places that have disappeared from the world's maps. In its pages, one will find lost empires and vanished kingdoms, cultures and societies that have faded from memory. Kings and great conquerors will appear and then dissolve into the past. Wars great and small will begin and end. Through it all, the Middle East will be revealed as a dynamic, vibrant, and exciting place in time.

Readers may use the map on the preceding page to plan their journey through the book's chapters. Each number corresponds to the chapter that deals with that particular location. This map and others scattered throughout the book will serve as a guide through time and space, from ancient days to the present in the region known as the Middle East.

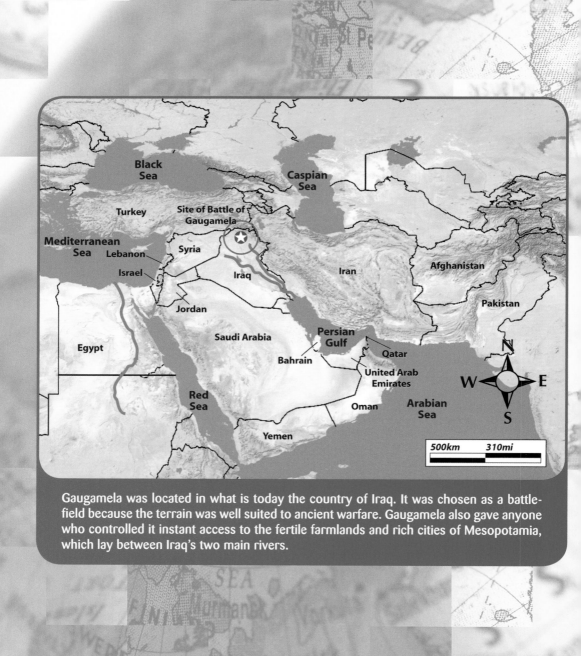

Black Sea

Caspian Sea

Turkey

Site of Battle of Gaugamela

Mediterranean Sea

Lebanon

Syria

Israel

Iraq

Iran

Afghanistan

Jordan

Pakistan

Egypt

Saudi Arabia

Persian Gulf

Qatar

Bahrain

United Arab Emirates

Red Sea

Oman

Arabian Sea

Yemen

N
W E
S

500km        310mi

Gaugamela was located in what is today the country of Iraq. It was chosen as a battle-field because the terrain was well suited to ancient warfare. Gaugamela also gave anyone who controlled it instant access to the fertile farmlands and rich cities of Mesopotamia, which lay between Iraq's two main rivers.

## Chapter 1

### The Plain of Gaugamela, 331 BCE

No one knew what was going through the young general's mind. He was just shy of his twenty-fifth birthday, and he had already conquered a large part of the ancient world. Now he stood face to face with one of the mightiest armies ever assembled. Darius III, king of Persia, had gathered together an awesome force. Some people said that he had a million men under his command. The actual number was probably far less, but Darius's army was still formidable.

His soldiers came from many places. There were Persians from what is modern-day Iran. Bactrians and Sogdianans from modern Afghanistan were there, too. Most of these troops were archers who either fought on foot, on horseback, or from chariots that had wicked-looking curved swords attached to their wheels. Darius also had some soldiers from India. He needed these men to work the fifteen armored elephants he planned to use in the upcoming fight. The king even had Greek mercenaries in his service. This was ironic considering the fact the Darius's young opponent that day in 331 BCE was a Greek himself. He came from Macedonia (maa-suh-DOH-nee-uh), the northernmost region of ancient Greece. His name was Alexander the Great.

The two sides met at the plain of Gaugamela (gaw-guh-MEE-luh). It was a long way from the rocky islands, craggy mountains, and golden fields of Greece. It had taken Alexander and his army three long years of marching and fighting to get there. During that time, the invaders had swept through the western half of the ancient Persian Empire. They conquered one Persian satrapy, or province, after another as they went. Eventually, a massive and diverse chunk of territory fell to the Greeks. When he finally brought Darius to battle, Alexander controlled what would become the modern countries of Turkey, Lebanon, Syria, Israel, Egypt, and part of Iraq. Vast mountain ranges, lush river valleys, and sandy seashores all belonged to the man who would someday conquer "nearly the whole of the known world in the name of Greek culture."[1]

Alexander's power would eventually stretch all the way to India, but first he had to take the plain of Gaugamela. It was a natural battlefield, and Alexander desperately wanted to possess it. Darius had very different ideas. He had already lost two major battles against the invaders from the West. Losing a third engagement, especially one so

Alexander the Great was easily recognizable to his enemies. He always wore fine golden armor and sat upon a stunning horse named Bucephalus.

deep in his own territory, would be a disaster. He had to hold fast at Gaugamela. For that reason, he had put a huge army in the field. He even had his engineers level the field of battle so his chariots could operate more effectively. The Persian king was determined to stop Alexander at all costs. If he didn't, the road to Darius's capital, Persepolis, would be wide open.

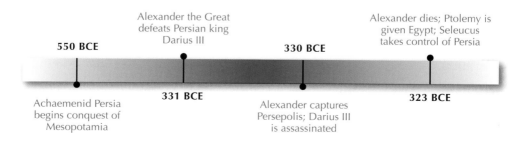

550 BCE

Alexander the Great defeats Persian king Darius III

330 BCE

Alexander dies; Ptolemy is given Egypt; Seleucus takes control of Persia

Achaemenid Persia begins conquest of Mesopotamia

331 BCE

Alexander captures Persepolis; Darius III is assassinated

323 BCE

Darius III, who fought against Alexander at Gaugamela, thought of himself as a ferocious warrior. In truth, he often abandoned his soldiers if defeat threatened.

On October 1, 331 BCE, Alexander moved to open that road. As Darius's army sat waiting for battle, Alexander marched out of his camp on the banks of the Tigris River. He told his men to be ready to "meet the enemy at dawn."[2] Alexander had perhaps 40,000 infantry and 7,000 cavalry under his command. Even if Darius did not have a million men, he certainly outnumbered the Macedonian Greeks.

Yet Alexander's troops were battle-hardened and fiercely loyal to their general, especially the small elite cavalry guard known as Alexander's Companions. His opponent could not make the same claim. The Persian army was multiethnic and multicultural, so its loyalties were often divided. Most of the soldiers fought for Darius only because they had to or, as with the Greek mercenaries, because they were paid to do so. Few Persian warriors felt personally attached to Darius, and he felt little responsibility to them.

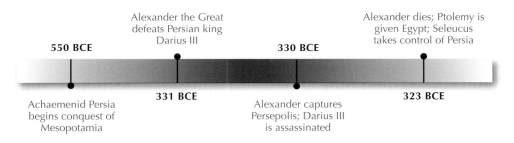

Alexander the Great defeats Persian king Darius III

Alexander dies; Ptolemy is given Egypt; Seleucus takes control of Persia

550 BCE

330 BCE

331 BCE

323 BCE

Achaemenid Persia begins conquest of Mesopotamia

Alexander captures Persepolis; Darius III is assassinated

Alexander's first prize after his victory at Gaugamela was the city of Babylon. As ancient as it was wealthy, the fabled city welcomed its new master.

Unevenly matched in more ways than one, the armies waited to fight. As the sun rose over Gaugamela, the differences between the two combatants came into focus. Darius's battle formations were gigantic but stiff and slow; Alexander's force was small but nimble. The Persian king put his elephants, fifty chariots, and Greek mercenaries in the middle of his array. Horsemen and units of archers, as well as two more groups of chariots, were set up to the right and left of Darius's personal cavalry at the head of the army. Persian infantry backed up the entire command.

Alexander arranged his troops into a single line, with cavalry and archers on its outside wings. He wanted to be sure that his defense would

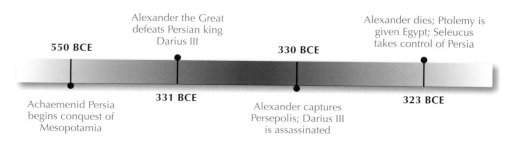

550 BCE

Alexander the Great
defeats Persian king
Darius III

330 BCE

Alexander dies; Ptolemy is
given Egypt; Seleucus
takes control of Persia

Achaemenid Persia
begins conquest of
Mesopotamia

331 BCE

Alexander captures
Persepolis; Darius III
is assassinated

323 BCE

have balance or, as an ancient historian wrote, so that "the front was not better secured than the flanks, nor the flanks better provided than the rear!"[3]

Feeling confident, Darius launched his assault, but everything went wrong from the start. His elephants panicked and proved worthless. Darius's chariots with their slashing bladed wheels did no damage at all. Alexander's men simply opened ranks and let them roll past, then turned and

Persepolis (per-SEH-puh-liss) was the capital of ancient Persia, but there were secondary capitals that the Persian kings often used. Susa and Ecbatana, both northwest of Persepolis, were the others.

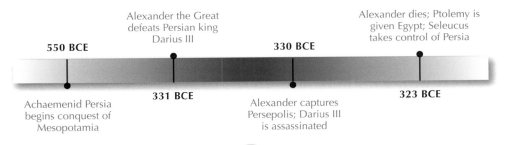

Alexander the Great
defeats Persian king
Darius III

Alexander dies; Ptolemy is
given Egypt; Seleucus
takes control of Persia

**550 BCE**

**330 BCE**

**323 BCE**

**331 BCE**

Achaemenid Persia
begins conquest of
Mesopotamia

Alexander captures
Persepolis; Darius III
is assassinated

The battle of Gaugamela sealed the fate of ancient Persia. Militarily and politically it was perhaps Alexander the Great's most important victory.

destroyed the vehicles one by one. The Persian cavalry charged again and again, but it could not break the Macedonian-Greek line. Soon the ground was slippery with blood, and the air was filled with the screams of wounded and dying men. Most of these cries came from Persian mouths.

With arrows filling the sky and the clanging of sword against sword filling men's ears, Alexander counterattacked. Shifting to the Persian left, Alexander forced an opening in the enemy lines and then galloped

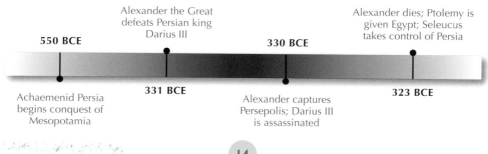

Alexander the Great
defeats Persian king
Darius III

Alexander dies; Ptolemy is
given Egypt; Seleucus
takes control of Persia

550 BCE

330 BCE

Achaemenid Persia
begins conquest of
Mesopotamia

331 BCE

Alexander captures
Persepolis; Darius III
is assassinated

323 BCE

through with his trusty Companions beside him. Once within the Persian ranks, the Macedonian king glimpsed a brightly colored and well-guarded tent on a low hill. The tent was the Persian command post. He made directly for it. Darius, frozen in fear, watched as Alexander fought his way closer. Then he did the only thing he could think of doing—he ran away.

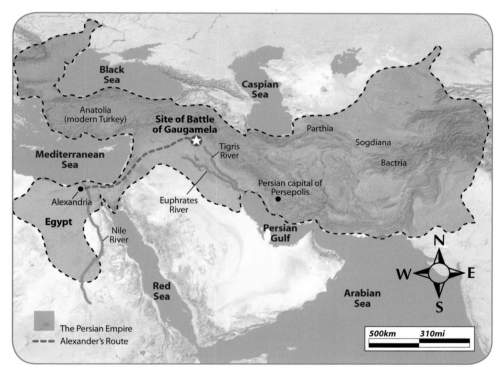

**The Persian Empire**
**- - - Alexander's Route**

In 331 BCE, after his bloodless occupation of Egypt, Alexander marched from Alexandria into the Persian heartland. His ultimate goal was to bring Darius's armies to a climactic battle.

Alexander the Great defeats Persian king Darius III

550 BCE

330 BCE

Alexander dies; Ptolemy is given Egypt; Seleucus takes control of Persia

Achaemenid Persia begins conquest of Mesopotamia

331 BCE

Alexander captures Persepolis; Darius III is assassinated

323 BCE

The Persian army was known for its mounted archers. They carried their bow and arrows in a saddle quiver located next to their sword.

Taking his personal bodyguards with him, Darius jumped into his chariot and speedily rode off, leaving his soldiers behind.

To its credit, the Persian army fought on for a while, but its defeat was now certain. Most of the troops fled; those who stayed were either captured or killed. The Macedonian-Greek casualties were in the hundreds; the Persian numbers were ten times that. Gaugamela was a royal slaughter and signaled the end of a Persian Empire that had been in existence for two centuries.

Alexander the Great's victory at Gaugamela opened the ancient Middle East to the Greek ideas that had already been reshaping the West. Art, science, literature, and politics over the entire region from modern Turkey to Pakistan would never be the same. In the words of historian Michael Grant, Alexander died in 323 BCE, "leaving the world transformed."[4]

Yet for all that, Gaugamela, the place of such an important battle, has been largely forgotten. The open plain is anonymous once more. Like so many other ancient places, from Mesopotamia (mess-uh-poh-TAY-mee-uh) to the Ottoman Empire, Gaugamela exists now only on maps from another time, maps of a world lost in history.

## Darius After Gaugamela

Persian kings were renowned for their willingness to retreat when it became clear that they could not defeat their enemies. Following this tradition, Darius III left the field at Gaugamela after he realized that he had lost. He took only a small guard force with him; he abandoned the rest of his army to the mercies of Alexander the Great.

This flight was nothing new for him. At the battle of Issus two years earlier, Darius had abandoned one of his wives, his mother, and several daughters to be taken by Alexander. Riding as quickly as he could, the Persian king fled in his chariot toward Persepolis, his capital city. The king arrived safely, but did not stay long. Alexander was sure to march on Persepolis to follow up after his victory, so Darius kept going. Much as he had run out on his soldiers at Gaugamela, Darius left his palace and family to be captured by the Macedonian Greeks. From Persepolis, the king rode northeast to the distant province of Bactria. He hoped that his old friend and former general Bessus would hide him. Bessus, however, had other ideas. He hoped to pull what was left of Persia together under his

Darius III had a well-earned reputation for leaving his soldiers when they needed him most. He also had a habit of abandoning family members to Alexander. Both at the battle of Issus and at Persepolis, Alexander took Darius's relatives captive.

rule. Bessus even thought he might be able to make a deal with Alexander. Of course, Darius would have to be out of the way for this to happen, so Bessus had the fugitive king murdered. When Alexander found out that Darius had been slain, he was furious; he had wanted to kill Darius himself. In retaliation, Alexander had Bessus hunted down and executed. Darius's body was later recovered by Macedonian soldiers and presented to Alexander. In a show of respect for his old enemy, he had the corpse sent back to Persepolis for a royal funeral and entombment.

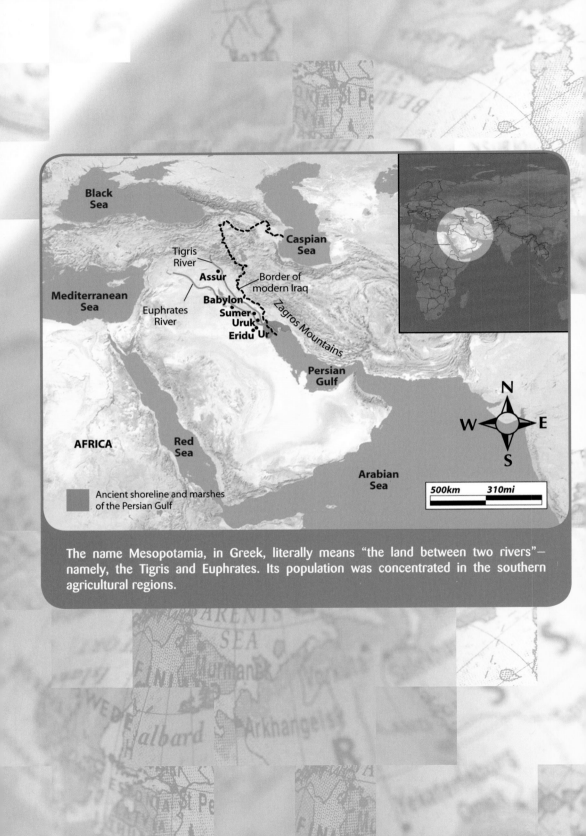

Black
Sea

Caspian
Sea

Tigris
River

Assur

Border of
modern Iraq

Mediterranean
Sea

Babylon

Euphrates
River

Sumer
Uruk

Eridu  Ur

Zagros Mountains

Persian
Gulf

N

W          E

S

AFRICA

Red
Sea

Arabian
Sea

Ancient shoreline and marshes
of the Persian Gulf

500km      310mi

The name Mesopotamia, in Greek, literally means "the land between two rivers"—
namely, the Tigris and Euphrates. Its population was concentrated in the southern
agricultural regions.

# Chapter 2

## Mesopotamia of Old

Not far from Gaugamela, the crystal blue waters of the Tigris River flow gently southward toward the Persian Gulf. Fed by small streams rushing out of the mountains of southeastern Turkey, the Tigris slows down as it reaches the flat expanses between the modern city of Baghdad and the ruins of the ancient city of Babylon. At this point, the river begins to drift closer to the Euphrates (yoo-FRAY-teez), its western companion that also has its source in the mountainous north.

Together, the Tigris and Euphrates look like a pair of outstretched arms, cradling a long unbroken ribbon of fertile ground between them. The soil there is rich and perfect for farming. Today, this river valley is in the country of Iraq, but many thousands of years ago the land was known as Mesopotamia.

By any name, it is a complex region. The climate differs greatly depending upon where one is. The mountains that represent its northern boundary are cold and snowy. The foothills are a bit warmer, with more rain than snow annually. Farther south, it becomes hot and dry, despite all the water carried by the twin rivers. Sandstorms are a common occurrence. In the far south, where the Tigris and Euphrates flow together to form a vast delta, the air hangs with humidity (moisture in the air), and warmth prevails year-round. The weather becomes almost tropical at the junction with the Persian Gulf.

The terrain also varies from one location to another. Barren, jagged mountains blend into rolling foothills covered in grasses. The hills then give way to table-flat deserts, studded with groves of palm trees and

The Tigris River (above), along with the Euphrates, made farming in Mesopotamia possible. Without the life-sustaining waters of these two rivers, agricultural development could not have taken place.

thickets of brush wherever water percolates up through the ground. Finally, where the rivers meet the sea, verdant marshlands are abundant.

The diversity of the natural world extends to people, too. Ethnic Kurds call the north home. Sunni (SOO-nee) Arabs, who began arriving in Mesopotamia in the seventh century, are clustered in the desert midlands. Arabs following the Shia (SHEE-ah) version of Islam predominate in the south, while people known as Marsh Arabs inhabit the soggy delta. Other

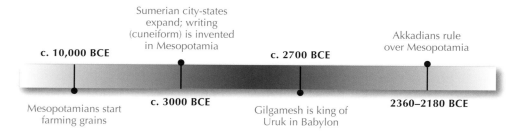

Sumerian city-states expand; writing (cuneiform) is invented in Mesopotamia

c. 10,000 BCE

c. 2700 BCE

Akkadians rule over Mesopotamia

Mesopotamians start farming grains

c. 3000 BCE

Gilgamesh is king of Uruk in Babylon

2360–2180 BCE

The plains of northern Mesopotamia were home to a variety of tribal peoples who had originated in the Zagros Mountains. Herders and nomads from these mountains were drawn to the flatlands by the gentle climate and the promise of an agricultural lifestyle.

groups are scattered throughout the modern Iraqi heartland. Many are descended from some of the earliest residents of the region, such as the Assyrians and Chaldeans (kal-DEE-unz).

Yet the place their ancestors knew did not resemble Iraq at all, politically speaking. Ancient Mesopotamia was not a single country. It was instead an often loose collection of city-states, which dotted the banks of the great rivers. These cities, which functioned as small kingdoms, evolved from towns which had themselves begun as scattered villages that popped up once people learned to farm.

c. 1800– c. 1600 BCE

Hammurabi produces written laws

c. 1600– c. 1200 BCE

Hittites invade Babylon

c. 900 BCE

c. 1780 BCE

Babylon dominates Mesopotamia

1531 BCE

The kingdoms of Mitanni and the Kassites rise and fall

Assyria enters its period of greatest territorial expansion

An old Mesopotamian legend spoke of a time when human beings "did not know of bread for eating or garments for wearing . . . they ate herbs with their mouths like sheep, [and] they drank ditch-water."[1] This situation began to change sometime around 12,000 years ago. People in Mesopotamia discovered a way to plant and harvest several varieties of grasses that grew naturally in the floodplains of the Tigris and Euphrates. They became the first farmers. No longer compelled to gather and hunt for their food, the Mesopotamians settled down and started cultivating grains such as wheat, barley, and rye that could be turned into bread.

For the first time in history, people had a surplus of food. This bounty allowed for rapid population growth and the division of labor. In other words, people began doing more and different kinds of jobs. All this new activity required novel forms of social and political organization. These began to develop around 2500 BCE.

By that date, powerful city-states, known collectively as Sumer (SOO-mur), had emerged in southern Mesopotamia. Centered on trade, manufacturing, and agriculture, these city-states were governed by kings and were almost like tiny independent countries. They shared a language (now dead) and a form of writing known as cuneiform (kyoo-NEE-uh-form), the world's first writing system. They also had in common a set of religious beliefs and practices and many social customs, but that was the extent of it. The people of early Mesopotamia did not sense any kinship. Indeed, they fought bitterly and often, especially the large and powerful Sumerian city-states such as Babylon, Eridu, Ur, and Uruk, home to the mythical hero-king Gilgamesh (GIL-guh-mesh).

Resilient and durable, the Sumerian city-states survived all the wars among themselves and numerous foreign invasions. Surprisingly, they actually prospered through it all, even when intruders imposed their rule.

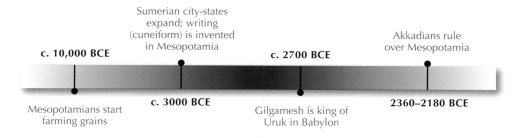

Sumerian city-states expand; writing (cuneiform) is invented in Mesopotamia

c. 10,000 BCE

c. 2700 BCE

Akkadians rule over Mesopotamia

Mesopotamians start farming grains

c. 3000 BCE

Gilgamesh is king of Uruk in Babylon

2360–2180 BCE

The first of these intruders were the Akkadians (uh-KAY-dee-unz). Northern Mesopotamian neighbors of the Sumerians, the Akkadians were a warlike people who spoke a language related to modern Hebrew and Arabic. They swept down between the Tigris and Euphrates sometime around the year 2360 BCE, led by their king, Sargon I. Sargon, an intelligent and brutal ruler, conquered the city-states one by one. No one stood in his way. Mesopotamia crumbled before him. "Sargon, King of Akkad," it was written, "subdued all its territory from Lagash to the sea."[2]

After taking his final prize, Sargon famously washed his weapons in the azure waters of the Persian Gulf and declared his new domain to be an empire; he thought that it would last forever. Following his example, Akkadian kings ruled over Sumer for more than two centuries.

Sargon I, shown here standing before the tree of life, united Mesopotamia under a single ruler. He is credited, by doing so, with having established the Western world's first empire—Akkadian Sumer.

The city-states proved too tough, though. They eventually regained their independence. They continued using the Akkadian language, which doomed native Sumerian to extinction. The notion of empire, however, once learned could not be unlearned.

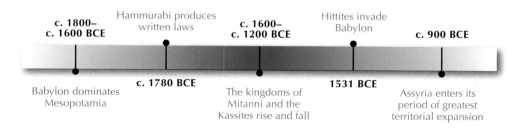

c. 1800– c. 1600 BCE — Babylon dominates Mesopotamia

Hammurabi produces written laws — c. 1780 BCE

c. 1600– c. 1200 BCE — The kingdoms of Mitanni and the Kassites rise and fall

Hittites invade Babylon — 1531 BCE

c. 900 BCE — Assyria enters its period of greatest territorial expansion

Near the end of the nineteenth century BCE, one of the city-states, Babylon, rose to power. Renowned for its urban splendor, Babylon was at the center of a vast breadbasket. Grain grew in abundance between the Tigris and Euphrates. Wealthy and well-fed, Babylon quickly extended its control over much of Mesopotamia. It soon bullied the other city-states into accepting its control over them.

Many changes came along with Babylonian domination. Perhaps the most important was the introduction of a written legal code. This code was the product of a single king named Hammurabi (ham-uh-ROB-ee), so it bears his name: the Code of Hammurabi. It was designed to unite Mesopotamia by directing every aspect of life and was quite specific as to crimes and their punishment. Composed before the invention of jails and prisons, the code prescribes fines as the most common punishment, but death is not far behind. In fact, death was not an uncommon penalty for crimes that today result only in prison sentences. For example, Hammurabi's

Hammurabi's stela is a column of diorite that stands eight feet tall. The top portion shows Hammurabi meeting with Shamash, Babylon's god of the sun and justice. Hammurabi's Code of Law is inscribed below in 49 columns of cuneiform.

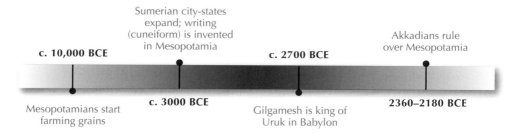

Sumerian city-states expand; writing (cuneiform) is invented in Mesopotamia

c. 10,000 BCE

c. 2700 BCE

Akkadians rule over Mesopotamia

Mesopotamians start farming grains

c. 3000 BCE

Gilgamesh is king of Uruk in Babylon

2360–2180 BCE

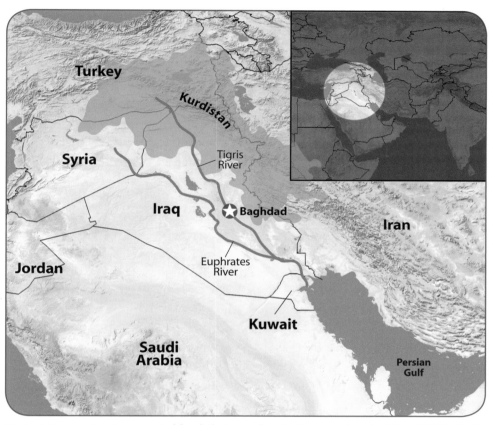

Ancient Mesopotamia occupied land that now lies in the very heart of the Middle East. Although many centuries have passed, the area is still known for its fertile farmland— and it still experiences more than its share of political turmoil and conflict.

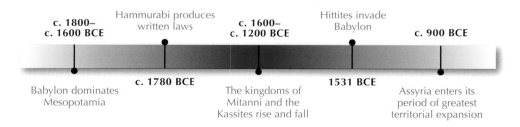

c. 1800– c. 1600 BCE

Hammurabi produces written laws

c. 1600– c. 1200 BCE

Hittites invade Babylon

c. 900 BCE

Babylon dominates Mesopotamia

c. 1780 BCE

The kingdoms of Mitanni and the Kassites rise and fall

1531 BCE

Assyria enters its period of greatest territorial expansion

code stated: "If anyone is committing a robbery and is caught, then he shall be put to death."[3]

After Sargon, Hammurabi was the second great king to try to unite Mesopotamia under a single ruler. Like so many others who would come after him, however, Hammurabi failed. Babylonian supremacy in Mesopotamia did not last. By 1531 BCE, Babylon collapsed under the weight of an invasion by the Hittites, a people who came from Anatolia (modern Turkey). The chaos of the next few decades opened Mesopotamia to foreign attack and domination by outsiders. For a long time, the Mesopotamians were subjects of foreign kings. A people called the Hurrians took over northern Mesopotamia, creating the kingdom of Mitanni. The Kassites, farm folk originating in modern Iran, occupied the southern part. And yet, the city-states survived. They kept some of their independence even under the watchful eyes of their Hurrian and Kassite overlords. In time, matters settled down, and people got used to the new political situation.

Just as they did, however, a new threat appeared. Fierce warriors from the area around the northern city of Assur (ah-SOOR) had begun to push southward. Native to the mountains on the upper fringes of Mesopotamia, these people were actually a blend of different ethnic groups. Still, they thought of themselves as Mesopotamians and for centuries had looked with envy on the gentle climate and rich farmlands of the south. Babylon's fall and its replacement by the comparatively weak Hurrians and Kassites gave the northerners an opportunity to expand. When they were done, Mesopotamia of old became the center of the world's first genuine international power—the empire of Assyria (uh-SEER-ee-uh).

## Gilgamesh, the Hero of Mesopotamia

"Gilgamesh, the vanguard and the rearguard of the army . . . two-thirds a god, one-third a man, the king."[4] That is how the Mesopotamians of old thought of the famous king of the city of Uruk, at least the legendary one. Historians and others believe that at one time Uruk was indeed governed by a king named Gilgamesh, and that his reign was one of security and prosperity for the people. The details of the real king Gilgamesh and his time on the throne have long since been forgotten, but he certainly never matched the awesome power of his fictitious namesake.

Long told orally, the epic of Gilgamesh was recorded by the Assyrians, who copied it from an earlier Sumerian text probably written in cuneiform and on clay tablets. It represents the world's first piece of true literature. No one knows the original source. Regardless, the story is the same. Burdened with the defense of his city, King Gilgamesh embarks on a series of adventures accompanied by his loyal friend, Enkidu (EN-kee-doo). Together they fight supernatural bulls, defy angry goddesses, and wander in search of immortality. When Enkidu dies sud-

A cuneiform tablet containing a small part of the epic of Gilgamesh. Originally meant to be presented orally, the story was written down on clay tablets perhaps 2,000 years after its first telling.

denly, Gilgamesh even journeys to the land of the dead. His search for eternal life eventually leads to his realization that being remembered for what one has accomplished is real immortality. In the end, Gilgamesh proves his worth to his people and goes down in history as Mesopotamia's champion.

Written over 2,000 years ago, the tale of Gilgamesh offers a glimpse inside a long-gone culture and society. The world described in the story no longer exists. Its voices, those of kings and common folk alike, have been silenced by the centuries. Gilgamesh now rules over a vanished realm, but every time his epic is told, the god-king fights again for his city and his honor. Reading about Gilgamesh's exploits transports the reader back to one of the many places in the Middle East that has been lost in time.

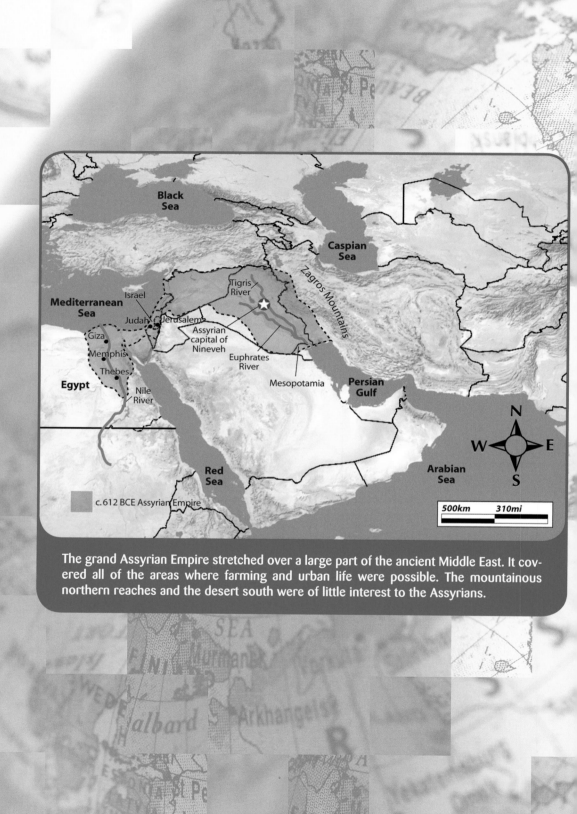

Black
Sea

Caspian
Sea

Zagros Mountains

Mediterranean
Sea

Israel

Judah

Jerusalem

Tigris
River

Assyrian
capital of
Nineveh

Euphrates
River

Mesopotamia

Persian
Gulf

Giza

Memphis

Thebes

Egypt

Nile
River

Red
Sea

Arabian
Sea

N

W     E

S

c. 612 BCE Assyrian Empire

500km          310mi

The grand Assyrian Empire stretched over a large part of the ancient Middle East. It covered all of the areas where farming and urban life were possible. The mountainous northern reaches and the desert south were of little interest to the Assyrians.

# Chapter 3

## Mighty Assyria

Along the upper reaches of the Tigris, where the mountains dissolve slowly into rolling hills and floodplains, the Western world's first great empire was born. Sandwiched between the kingdoms of the Mitanni and the Kassites, the cities of Assur, Nineveh (NIH-nuh-vuh), and Arbela (ar-BEE-luh) began as small village communities. They quickly grew into city-states and came to dominate the land that became Assyria. No one could have predicted the spectacular history that would follow. People at the time could not have imagined how strong Assyria would become. Nor could they have foreseen the incredible rise and eventual fall of the first in a long line of empires that tried to dominate the region we call the Middle East.

The Assyrians, like their Mesopotamian neighbors, started out as peaceful farmers and herdsmen. Over time, as settlements evolved into villages and then into towns, small-scale manufacturing and craft production grew up. The Assyrians, then, followed a common course of development, and should have come to resemble other peoples in the region more closely.

Yet their homeland differed sharply from other parts of Mesopotamia. Cool summers and wet chilly winters were the rule in the foothills of southern Assyria; deep snows often blanketed the northern mountains. The climate and terrain of Assyria were more demanding and less forgiving than elsewhere, so the inhabitants took on the same qualities. More than one ancient observer claimed that the weather and land "served to toughen their fiber [and] gradually harden them into the form which they bore during all their history."[1] Assyrians adapted to their surroundings by

**The Assyrians were skilled warriors. They had mastered the use of powerful bows and battering rams.**

embracing a warrior tradition and integrating horses into their culture. An outlook built around war and a lifestyle based on horses became key parts of what it meant to be Assyrian. Both would contribute to Assyria's invincibility—for a while, anyway.

Assyria's population began to expand around the year 2000 BCE. The expansion was made possible by the continual increase in the amount of land under cultivation. Assyria's material wealth increased as well. One reason was that the mountains of the north held large amounts of copper. This metal was in constant demand for use in tools and weapons.

**c. 3000 BCE**

Small-scale manufacturing and craft production arise in Assyria

**c. 2000 BCE**

Cities of Assur, Nineveh, and Arbela begin as small villages

**c. 2500 BCE**

Assyria's population begins to outgrow its borders in northern Mesopotamia

Outgrowing their homeland and feeling aggressive, the Assyrians looked beyond their borders for more space and resources. The fertile land and rich cities between the Tigris and Euphrates naturally drew their attention. So the Assyrians, beginning around the year 1200 BCE, pushed slowly but steadily into the Mesopotamian heartland. Along the way, Assyria provoked a long war with Babylon. Next came the rest of Sumer, then the Kassites to the east. Not long afterward, the kingdom of Mitanni was swallowed up by Assyria. Up and down the valley of the Tigris and Euphrates and into the mountains beyond, the Assyrians conquered and absorbed every opponent.

Assyria was now ready to expand into places no Mesopotamian power had ever dreamed of going. Assyrian armies pierced the western mountains and swept toward the coast of the Mediterranean Sea, a destination the Assyrians called "the upper ocean of the setting sun."[2] As they went, the Assyrians captured city after city and erased kingdom after kingdom. Each time, wealth and food flowed back to the Assyrian homeland and its capital at Nineveh. Phoenicia (fih-NEE-shee-uh), Philistia (fih-LISS-tee-uh), and Canaan (KAY-nun), places that no longer appear on maps of the Middle East, surrendered to Assyrian rule. Led by fierce warrior-kings, the Assyrians defeated every enemy and took whatever they wanted. People at the time spoke of Assyria as a "bird of prey [that] filled the world with blood."[3]

The Assyrian victories resulted not only from solid fighting skills and sheer ferocity but also from high technology—high technology for those days, at least. Assyrian soldiers carried powerful bows that could be fired from horseback as well as on foot. In fact, the Assyrians were some of the first troops to fight from horses; they used cavalry to a greater extent than anyone before them. These same bows could also be combined with the tried-and-true chariot to enable the Assyrians to employ unique and very

c. 1200 BCE

Assyria enters its period of greatest territorial expansion

858–824 BCE

Assyrians push slowly into the Mesopotamian heartland

c. 900 BCE

Shalmaneser III rules Assyria

effective tactics that blended speed and firepower. Backing up the Assyrian frontline troops were engineers trained in the construction of elaborate siege equipment such as battle towers and battering rams, which allowed the Assyrians to take most of the walled cities they encountered with ease.

Kings of unrivaled competence commanded the Assyrian forces. Shalmaneser (shall-muh-NEE-zur) III and Tiglathpileser (tig-lath-puh-LEE-zur) III began the imperial expansion of Assyria in the ninth and eighth centuries BCE. They conquered huge tracts of land for the empire. Babylon finally fell in 731 BC. Sargon II, known for his fierce determination, took credit for the destruction of Israel, one of the two ancient Jewish kingdoms. Israel was a commercial kingdom, known for its bustling cities and towns and for the extent of its religious tolerance. In 720 BCE, its capital, Samaria (suh-MAYR-ee-uh), fell to the advancing Assyrians, who destroyed the city and sent its inhabitants back to Assyria as forced laborers. The Old Testament of the Bible attributed the disaster to the fact that the

Everyone conquered by the Assyrians was forced to pay tribute and homage to the Assyrian kings. This included the Israelites, shown in this drawing coming before king Shalmanezer III.

745–727 BCE

Babylon falls to
Tiglathpileser III

720 BCE

Tiglathpileser III
rules Assyria

731 BCE

Israel falls to Assyrian
king Sargon II

Israelites made "a great sin." God consequently punished Israel by removing it "out of his sight. . . . So was Israel carried away out of their own land to Assyria unto this day."[4]

Nineteen years later, another Assyrian king, Sennacherib (suh-NAK-uh-rub), bullied Judah, the other Jewish kingdom, into submission. After a long but unsuccessful siege of Jerusalem, the Assyrians accepted a Judahite offer of ransom and left. Judah was one of the few states along the Mediterranean coast to escape destruction. The biblical account of the war claims that Judah survived due to direct intervention of the Jewish God. He was said to have promised the people of Jerusalem that the vast army outside its walls would never enter their fortress: "the king of Assyria shall not come into the city. . . . For I will defend this city."[5] Whether preserved by the hand of God or not, Jerusalem held out. The Assyrians moved on and left Judah intact.

Egypt was less fortunate. Moving southward toward the fertile Nile valley, the Assyrians aimed to conquer the land of the pharaohs. A place of awesome beauty and majesty, Egypt was also rich in grain and other foodstuffs that could help feed an ever larger and ever hungrier Assyrian empire.

Sweeping in from the north, through the dense, reed-choked Nile Delta, the Assyrian army methodically worked its way down the timeless river. The ancient and sacred city of Memphis, near the Great Pyramids of Giza, was captured in 671 BCE. Seven years later, under the command of the famous king Ashurbanipal (ah-shoor-BAH-nuh-pahl), the Assyrians entered and looted Thebes (THEEBS). Thebes was the heart of classical Egypt. When it fell, a proud land and people belonged to the Assyrians.

The middle of the seventh century BCE saw Assyria ruling over an immense territory that covered all of Mesopotamia, the Mediterranean coast, and Egypt. No ancient power had ever controlled so vast an area.

Assyrians capture Giza, Egypt

701 BCE    664 BCE

Assyrians fail to take Jerusalem; Judah becomes tributary to Assyria

671 BCE

Assyrians take Thebes; Egypt falls

The Assyrians, militarily and politically, were the unquestioned masters of the Middle East. Under their banner, diverse cultures and societies jostled with one another. For the first time, a multitude of peoples had been brought together within a single political state.

The Assyrians, however, proved to be better at conquering places than running them. They struggled to keep their empire in one piece and were forced to stamp out endless small uprisings. The cities and kingdoms under their rule expected the Assyrians to manage their affairs and solve

The Nile River was crucial to ancient Egyptian society, culture, and economy. Its waters allowed farmers to irrigate their fields while providing a highway for trade and travel between Upper (southern) and Lower (northern) Egypt.

Babylon falls to
Tiglathpileser III

**745–727 BCE**

**720 BCE**

**731 BCE**

Tiglathpileser III
rules Assyria

Israel falls to Assyrian
king Sargon II

their problems. In short, they expected their imperial rulers to set up an empire, but the Assyrians were not up to the task. They were incredibly clumsy at handling the day-to-day administration of the occupied territories. The Assyrians let their empire drift, preferring to assert themselves through minor wars and local strongmen.

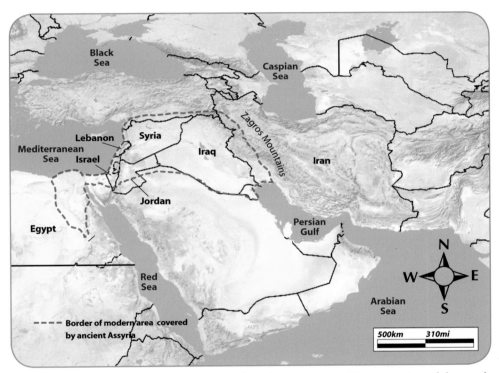

The Assyrian Empire encompassed or bordered upon many of the countries of the modern Middle East. Today's nation of Syria, however, was an outlying part. The imperial homeland was in Iraq.

701 BCE

Assyrians capture
Giza, Egypt

664 BCE

Assyrians fail to take
Jerusalem; Judah becomes
tributary to Assyria

671 BCE

Assyrians take Thebes;
Egypt falls

The Pyramids of Giza are some of the most easily recognized structures on earth. They are named for the kings for whom they were constructed—(left to right) Menkaure, Khafre, and Khufu.

The Assyrian kings could not be faulted for losing track of their foreign affairs. Their subjects in the territories and their client states were a quarrelsome lot, and there seemed to be no easy way to rule such a huge chunk of the Middle East. And then there was the immigration problem. Immigrants from the Zagros (ZAG-russ) Mountains, along Assyria's eastern frontier, were filtering into Mesopotamia at an alarming rate. These were foreigners with different customs, beliefs, and languages. They came in groups large and small and made their home in Assyria. Then they brought the empire crashing down.

## The Assyrians at Jerusalem—According to the Bible

Archaeological evidence confirms the fact that the armies of the Assyrian empire rampaged along the shores of the eastern Mediterranean in the early years of the eighth century BCE. From modern Lebanon to Egypt, Assyrian soldiers took over one city after another. During the course of a type of military campaign the ancient Middle East had never seen, they brought down multiple kingdoms. One of those kingdoms was Israel, which fell in 720 BCE. Israel was a prosperous, sophisticated, and cosmopolitan state that prided itself on religious tolerance. It also felt confident in its defenses. Here, it was wrong. Its defenses were no match for the Assyrians. They swept in from the north around the year 730 BCE, and quickly overran the tiny country. Israel's neighbor to the south, Judah, turned out to be more enduring. The Assyrians tried to do to Judah what they had done to Israel, but they failed to conquer it. After some initial success, the Assyrians laid siege to the city of Jerusalem. Every other city they had encircled had fallen, but Jerusalem held out stubbornly. Eventually, the Assyrians relented, lifted their siege, and moved on to less feisty opponents.

If the Judahites are to be believed, it was divine intervention that saved Jerusalem; they claimed God delivered them from the Assyrians: "And it came to pass . . . that the angel of the Lord went out and [killed] in the camp of the Assyrians an hundred fourscore and five thousand, and when [the Judahites] arose early in the morning, [the Assyrians] were all dead corpses. So Sennacherib king of Assyria departed . . ."[6]

Many historians disagree. They say that the Judahites purchased their salvation by agreeing to pay tribute to the Assyrians.

The ancient Judahites believed that God himself, by sending an angel, saved them from the Assyrians. Angels are often portrayed in religious art as vengeful warriors.

Like so many other local kings who wanted to avoid the wrath of the Assyrians, the Judahite king, Hezekiah (heh-zuh-KY-uh), paid them to go away. From that point on, Judah would have been what was known as a tribute state. This meant that the Judahites' freedom depended upon paying a sum of money every year to the Assyrians.

In any case, the story of Jerusalem's defense became a core component of the biblical tradition of divine intervention. It created a storyline in which God could be depended upon to rescue his chosen people from foreign foes.

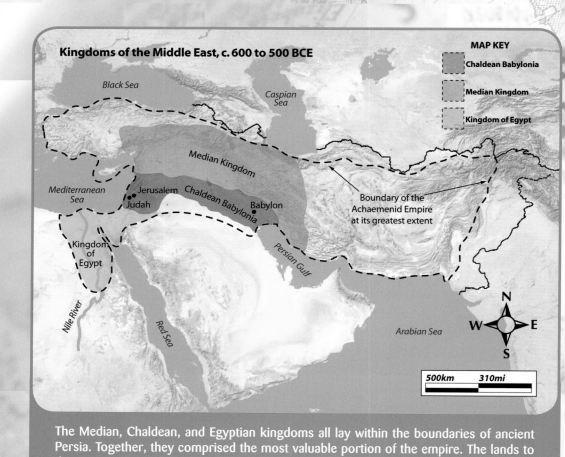

## Kingdoms of the Middle East, c. 600 to 500 BCE

**MAP KEY**

Chaldean Babylonia

Median Kingdom

Kingdom of Egypt

Black Sea

Caspian Sea

Median Kingdom

Jerusalem  Chaldean Babylonia
Judah                         Babylon

Boundary of the
Achaemenid Empire
at its greatest extent

Mediterranean
Sea

Kingdom
of
Egypt

Nile River

Red Sea

Persian Gulf

Arabian Sea

N
W        E
S

500km        310mi

The Median, Chaldean, and Egyptian kingdoms all lay within the boundaries of ancient Persia. Together, they comprised the most valuable portion of the empire. The lands to the east were sparsely inhabited mountains and deserts.

# Chapter 4

## Chaldeans and Achaemenids

The Assyrians were a warrior people. In their heyday, they thrived on battle and conquest. The masters of the Middle East took pride in their weapons and their skill at using them. Assyrian spears, bows, and horses allowed them to build an empire. Even in their spare time, the Assyrians practiced the arts of violence; their favorite pastime was hunting. Their kings, in fact, boasted more often of their hunting prowess than their military victories. One bragged that he had "killed 450 mighty lions and I slew 390 wild beasts. . . . I brought down 250 ostriches as if [they were] birds in a cage."[1] It seems fitting, then, that the Assyrian world collapsed amid the confusion of war, in bloodshed and invasion. As the Assyrians lived, so they died.

The end of Assyrian rule came suddenly in the year 612 BCE. After only a few years of warfare, the capital of Nineveh was taken and burned by a powerful coalition of three groups: the Medes (MEEDZ), Chaldeans, and Persians. The assault was brutal: "Horsemen charging, flashing sword and glittering spear, hosts of slain, heaps of corpses, dead bodies without end—they stumble over the bodies."[2]

The fact that all three of these groups had originally come from border regions far from the Tigris and Euphrates did not matter. The Mesopotamian heartland had long experienced repeated migrations from distant lands. Most of the immigrants belonged to mountain tribes that came from the northern and eastern ranges or the southern plains of Iran. Some tribes drifted in peacefully; others stormed in as invaders. All caused difficulties of one kind or another for the current inhabitants.

# Chapter 4

The palace of Sennacherib in Nineveh was a magnificent structure. Assyrian kings demanded that such places reflect their glory. The capital was destroyed in 612 BCE.

So it was in the seventh century BCE. The Medes, a people renowned for the quality of their horses, many of which were sold to the Assyrians, had lived a tribal existence until the Assyrians expanded into the Zagros Mountains. After that, many Medes remained in the mountains, but some settled along the upper Tigris River. They joined the Chaldeans, who had arrived several centuries earlier, and the Persians, who had originated in the coastal regions of southern Iran.

Living quietly at first, these groups over time grew restless and dissatisfied with Assyrian rule. Eventually they combined forces and attacked their overlords. The Assyrians, already weakened by the burden of maintaining an empire, could not put up an effective resistance. The new-

Nineveh is destroyed

**612 BCE**

**612 BCE**

**612 BCE**

Medes, Chaldeans, and Persians overthrow Assyria

Territory is redivided: Media (includes the Persians), Babylonia, Egypt

comers defeated the Assyrian armies and took over their cities, one by one. The end came when Nineveh was destroyed, and the victors immediately carved up the Assyrian empire.

The Medes created a unified kingdom, which ruled Medes and Persians alike. The Chaldeans established themselves in Babylon and began a project to revive the ancient kingdom once built around that city. They even took the name Babylonian as their own. The native governors of Assyrian Egypt, freed from foreign domination, established an independent monarchy and political state.

Although the Medes, Chaldeans, and Persians sought to put themselves in command of the former Assyrian empire, Chaldean Babylon soon emerged as the most powerful of the new kingdoms. The Chaldean Babylonians worked hard to create a new land reminiscent of the one ruled by the great Hammurabi more than a millennium earlier. They rebuilt much of the city of Babylon and restored its grandeur, making it a center of business, art, and learning. Under Chaldean administration, Babylon drew merchants, scholars, and craftsmen from far and wide. The city became famous for its temples, palaces, and gardens. In fact, the famous Hanging Gardens of Babylon was listed as one of the Seven Wonders of the World. The surrounding farmland was so bountiful that Greek historian Herodotus commented, "Of all the countries that we know, there is none so fruitful in grain . . . Babylonia must seem incredible to those who have not visited the country."[3] So many different languages were spoken in Babylon that the city hummed with diverse conversations. Some scholars believe that the English word *babble*, for a confused jumble of words, refers to multilingual Babylon.

The Chaldeans also pursued a policy of territorial expansion. Chaldean armies conquered much of the Euphrates floodplain before driving over the western mountains. Led by the shrewd and aggressive King

The Chaldean Babylonians capture Jerusalem

c. 600 BCE

587 BCE

Nebuchadnezzar II builds the Hanging Garden of Babylon

587 BCE

The Babylonian Exile of the Jews begins (lasts until 539 BCE)

Babylon was renowned for its architectural wonders, such as the Tower of Babel (background) and Hanging Gardens (foreground). Neither structure has survived from ancient times, and artists can only imagine what they looked like. Many ancient peoples associated Babylon with art and learning.

Nebuchadnezzar (neh-buh-kud-NEH-zur), the Chaldean Babylonians launched military campaigns against the city-states and minor kingdoms clustered along the shores of the eastern Mediterranean. Among these victims of Chaldean expansionism was Judah, which was taken in 587 BCE. The "Babylonian Exile" described in the Old Testament began

Nineveh is destroyed

**612 BCE**

**612 BCE**

**612 BCE**

Medes, Chaldeans, and Persians overthrow Assyria

Territory is redivided: Media (includes the Persians), Babylonia, Egypt that year, after Nebuchadnezzar ordered that a large part of the Judahite population be resettled in Babylonia. "So Judah was carried away out of their land," the Bible records, and into mass captivity.[4]

Although it began as a forced march into a foreign land, the Exile turned out to be a significant and not altogether negative development. Modern Judaism was born during this time. Exposure to different beliefs in Babylon allowed the centuries-old religion of Israel and Judah to mature. What started out as a local cult worshiping a

Nebuchadnezzar's role in spiriting the Jews into captivity, during the Babylonian Exile, made him a dark and reviled figure in biblical history. In this painting by William Blake, the king is depicted as an animal representing the sinfulness of humankind.

single god evolved into a full-fledged religion that would change history. Babylon was the venue for that transition.

Babylon did indeed soar to the heights of power during the early sixth century BCE. Yet despite the victories and accomplishments of its kings and people, Babylonian domination of the Middle East was brief. Within seventy-five years, Babylon was itself conquered.

Throughout the late seventh and early sixth centuries BCE, Persia had been growing in size and influence. It was soon able to gain control of the kingdom of Media (MEE-dee-uh) and then turn south into Babylonia. The Chaldeans could not match the Persians in the quality of their soldiers and generals. Under Persian attack, the outlying Babylonian cities fell. Then, in 539 BCE, Cyrus (SY-russ) the Great, a descendant of the very first Persian king, Achaemenes (ah-KEE-muh-neez) I, entered the city of

The Chaldean Babylonians capture Jerusalem

c. 600 BCE — 587 BCE

587 BCE

Nebuchadnezzar II builds the Hanging Garden of Babylon

The Babylonian Exile of the Jews begins (lasts until 539 BCE)

Babylon itself. With Media and Babylonia bowing down to this authority, Cyrus proclaimed a new Persian empire encompassing all of Mesopotamia and the Mediterranean coastal region. He also initiated a line of kings known as the Achaemenids (ah-KEE-muh-nudz). Achaemenid Persia had come into being.

Emboldened by their conquest of Mesopotamia, the Persians moved northward along the Tigris and Euphrates rivers and subdued the tribes of Kurdistan. Crossing the steep, snow-capped Kurdish mountains, the Persians swooped down into ancient Anatolia, in present-day Turkey, conquering the kingdoms of Gordia and Lydia. Moving farther west, the Persians

The Babylonian Exile was hard on the Jews, and many longed to return to their ancestral homeland.

came into contact with the Greek city-states of Ionia (eye-OH-nee-uh). Up to this point, the Persians had heard only vague reports of the Greeks, but now they actually met.

After absorbing Anatolia and pushing up against the Ionian Greeks, the Achaemenid armies plunged southward, hugging the shores of the blue Mediterranean. Phoenicia, with its superb harbors and rich cities, surrendered. From this place, the Persians would gather up the sailors

**550 BCE**

Persians take Kurdistan and Gordia, plus Lydia in Anatolia

**539 BCE**

Achaemenid Persia
begins its conquest
of Mesopotamia

**547 BCE**

Persians conquer
Phoenicia and Babylon

and ships that would help them put together the ancient world's most fearsome navy.

Next, the remnants of Judah were taken over. The Persians resettled the people who had been swept away by Nebuchadnezzar. The new Judah became a Persian province called Yehud (yeh-HOOD); its inhabitants

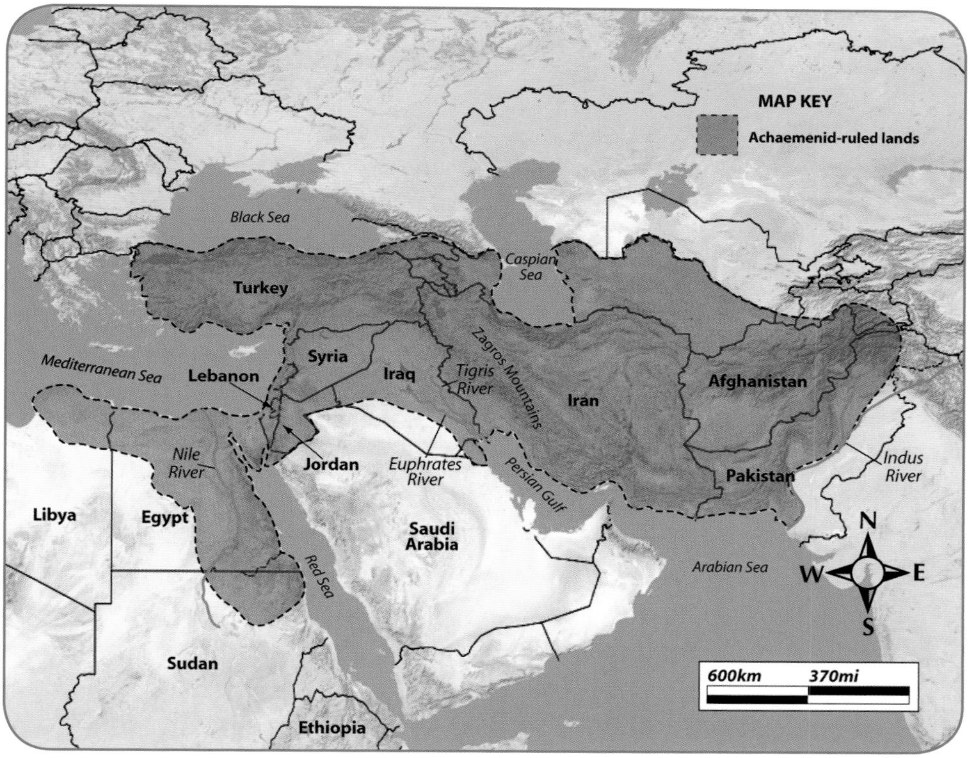


**Most of the modern Middle East came under Persian rule in ancient times. Even part of Pakistan nominally belonged to the Achaemenids.**

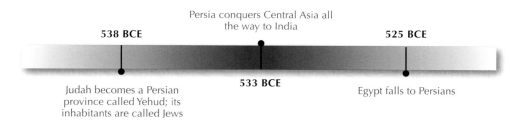

**538 BCE** — Judah becomes a Persian province called Yehud; its inhabitants are called Jews

**533 BCE** — Persia conquers Central Asia all the way to India

**525 BCE** — Egypt falls to Persians

The prophet Jeremiah is said to have warned the people of Jerusalem of Nebuchadnezzar's coming. Few listened, and the city paid dearly for it.

became known as the Jews. The days of religious persecution were over. Indeed, as a modern historian of Persia has noted, "tolerance of foreign religions was one of the most enlightened features of Persian rule."[5]

With the Mediterranean coast firmly in hand, the Achaemenid troops drove into the Nile valley. In 525 BCE, the Persians grabbed Egypt for themselves. The Land of the Black Soil, a reference to Egypt's fertile farmland, became the property of a line of kings from Mesopotamia.

As busy in the east as they were in the west, the Persians invaded Parthia, Bactria, Sogdiana, and a host of other Central Asian kingdoms. Eventually, the Achaemenids extended their reach all the way to the borders of India. Only at the Indus River did their soldiers halt, unwilling to challenge the war elephants of the Indian princes.

By the beginning of the fifth century BCE, the Persian Empire encompassed an area that included most of their known world. Persia's domination was unchallenged. As one modern writer put it, the "Persian kings had won for themselves and their people the largest empire ever seen . . . a multi-ethnic, multi-cultural, world-spanning state."[6] No empire had ever been as large or as strong. The Achaemenid monarchs reigned supreme. That is, until a young king from Macedonia came along with a small but devoted army and wiped Persia from the map.

## The Babylonian Exile and One God

The early Hebrews, who eventually split into Israelites and Judahites, are often credited with giving the world the concept of monotheism (mah-noh-THEE-izm), the idea that only one god exists in heaven. Most people in the ancient world worshiped many gods, a practice known as polytheism, so the Hebrews would appear to have been unique. In reality, the Hebrews were not technically monotheistic and, therefore, not as different from their neighbors as people might think.

The very earliest followers of the Hebrew god called him Yahweh (YAH-way), and they worshiped no others. The Hebrews did not, however, deny the existence of other deities; they just did not offer prayers to them. This is called monolatry (muh-NAH-luh-tree), or praying to only one god among the many that might be out there. Only after the Babylonian Exile, the period of more than forty years that the Hebrews spent in Mesopotamia, did the people of Yahweh claim that they bowed down before the only true God.

In the Bible, the first reference to genuine monotheism does not appear until the Book of Isaiah, which was written *after* the Exile. There, Yahweh proclaims, "I am the first, and I am the last, and beside me there is no God."[7] The explanation for the change lies in the Judahites' exposure to new religious ideas in Babylonia. The Eastern religion Zoroastrianism (zor-uh-WAS-tree-uh-nih-zum), popular in the region, most likely passed along the notion of one god to the unwilling guests from Judah who were then living in Babylonia.

In Zoroastrianism, there is only one god, a god of light, who constantly battles with the forces of darkness and evil in an effort to save humanity from everlasting torment.

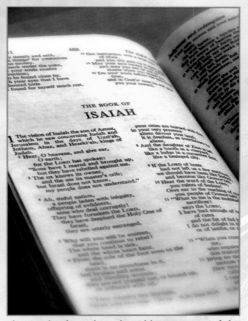

The Book of Isaiah in the Old Testament of the Bible

This god of light will eventually triumph, bringing peace and happiness to the world. Not only did this tradition inform Jewish monotheism, but it also became a central part of the Christian belief system.

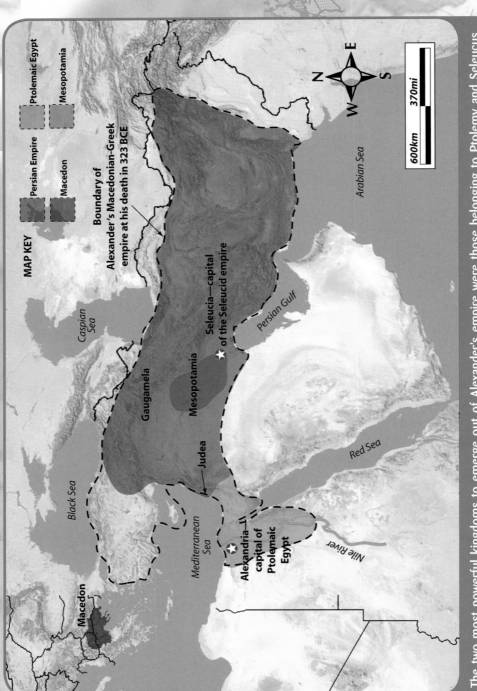

## MAP KEY

| | |
|---|---|
| Persian Empire | Ptolemaic Egypt |
| Macedon | Mesopotamia |

Boundary of Alexander's Macedonian-Greek empire at his death in 323 BCE

Macedon

Black Sea

Caspian Sea

Gaugamela

Mesopotamia

Seleucia—capital of the Seleucid empire

Judea

Mediterranean Sea

Alexandria— capital of Ptolemaic Egypt

Nile River

Red Sea

Persian Gulf

Arabian Sea

N E S W

600km 370mi

The two most powerful kingdoms to emerge out of Alexander's empire were those belonging to Ptolemy and Seleucus. Although the Seleucid Empire appears much larger, only its western portion was of much value to the Seleucid kings. Even then, Ptolemaic Egypt was far wealthier.

# Chapter 5

## Alexander's Empire and Beyond

Achaemenid Persia was more than a military powerhouse. It was sophisticated and cultured, too. Its marvelous cities were justly regarded as centers of art, science, and philosophy. Heavily urbanized for its time, Persia was a crossroads of global trade. Its capital, Persepolis, buzzed with commercial activity. Among the many achievements of the Achaemenid kings was the creation of a government that welcomed diversity and stressed ethnic tolerance and multiculturalism. In religion, Persia developed an early version of monotheism that influenced both Judaism and, later, Christianity. Zoroastrianism, the Persian religion, changed the way people thought of God and the afterlife.

Yet in many ways the empire was weak and vulnerable. The Persian economy was unstable and did not always guarantee a high standard of living. The diversity of the empire's population was the source of a good deal of tension. Sometimes the friction between differing cultural groups flared into violence. The Persian government was decentralized and never really asserted its authority in all parts of the empire. Worse still, the Persian kings were obsessed with the idea of conquering the Greek city-states. These city-states were like miniature kingdoms centered on individual Greek cities. Persia was an imperial state, so its kings were disdainful of independent cities. The Persians believed that everyone owed loyalty and obedience to the king.

Twice the Persians tried to invade the Greek peninsula. In 490 BCE, Darius I sent an army to Greece, an army that was handily defeated by the Athenians and their ally, Plataea (pluh-TEE-uh), at the battle of Marathon. Ten years later, Darius's son, Xerxes (ZERK-seez), sought to avenge

**Darius I was determined to conquer Greece and humble its people. Neither he nor any of his descendants accomplished that feat.**

his father's defeat by attacking Greece with a far larger force. He lost as well. This time around, the Greeks won battles on land and at sea, victories that convinced the Persians that any further attempts to subdue the Westerners would be foolish. Persian "kingship itself and all its power are dead," the victorious Greeks crowed.[1] After the Persian armies left Greece in 479 BCE, they never returned.

The next conflict between the Greeks and the Persians was played out in reverse. Nearly a century and a half later, Alexander the Great led an army into Persia. Son of Philip II, the Macedonian king who united the Greek city-states for the first time under a single ruler, Alexander took the throne in 336 BCE. He immediately began planning a war of conquest against Persia. Alexander wanted revenge for the earlier Persian expeditions against Greece, and he needed to gain legitimacy among a Greek people suspicious of Macedonian intentions. Alexander had to do something to make himself a real king; conquering Persia would certainly do that.

At any rate, the young monarch's temperament was suited for war. He was naturally aggressive, and his father had taught him to see honor in battle. Like other Macedonians, Alexander had been toughened by a

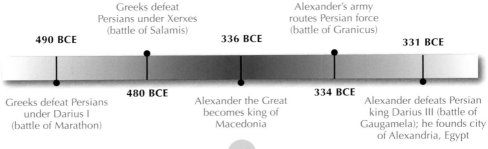

Greeks defeat Persians under Xerxes (battle of Salamis)

490 BCE

Alexander's army routes Persian force (battle of Granicus)

336 BCE

331 BCE

480 BCE

Greeks defeat Persians under Darius I (battle of Marathon)

334 BCE

Alexander the Great becomes king of Macedonia

Alexander defeats Persian king Darius III (battle of Gaugamela); he founds city of Alexandria, Egypt

harsh climate, hard work, and a culture that exalted combat. He loved horses and fighting. Alexander read everything he could, especially books on history and war. In every way, he worked to become a true leader.

Rugged and determined, Alexander looked forward to the invasion of Persia. In 334 BCE, his army crossed into Persian territory and routed a force sent to stop him at the battle of Granicus (gruh-NY-kuss).

The battle of Marathon was ancient Persia's first major military defeat before the war with Alexander. Few could have predicted that the Greeks could have fought so skillfully and with enough determination to turn back Darius I's invasion force.

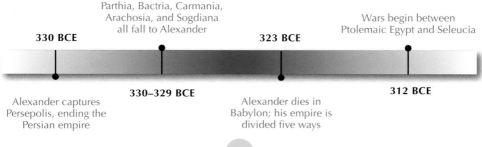

**330 BCE**

**323 BCE**

Parthia, Bactria, Carmania, Arachosia, and Sogdiana all fall to Alexander

Wars begin between Ptolemaic Egypt and Seleucia

**330–329 BCE**

**312 BCE**

Alexander captures Persepolis, ending the Persian empire

Alexander dies in Babylon; his empire is divided five ways

From there, the Macedonian-Greek army swept down along the coast of what is today Turkey. After crushing another Persian contingent at the battle of Issus the following year, this one led personally by Darius III, Alexander overran Phoenicia, Philistia, and Judea, home of the Jews. Nothing distracted him. When Darius offered to make peace, Alexander's top general, Parmenio (par-MEE-nee-oh), urged him to say yes: "If I were Alexander, I should accept." Brushing his suggestion aside, Alexander reminded his general that he spoke to no ordinary man. "And so should I," the king scoffed, "if I were Parmenio."[2]

He then marched into Egypt unopposed. The young king was now at the height of his power. No Persian army had been able to slow Alexander's progress, let alone defeat him on the battlefield. Every city and province in the western Persian Empire surrendered to him. While in Egypt, an oracle (a person who issues prophecies) took notice of his monumental achievements and told Alexander he was a god!

God or not, Alexander left Egypt confident in his prospects for total victory over Persia. He left behind a new multinational kingdom centered on Alexandria, the city the king had constructed in his own honor. Moving eastward, Alexander at last met the main Persian army at Gaugamela and defeated Darius for the third and final time. After his win, Alexander pursued his beaten foe to Persepolis, capturing the imperial capital in 330 BCE. A Macedonian Greek now sat on the throne of Persia; the Achaemenids were no more.

Darius slipped out of Persepolis before Alexander arrived; however, the Persian king's days as a fugitive were numbered. Just as Alexander was leaving Persepolis, he received news of Darius's assassination at the hands of a traitorous Bactrian general. It did not matter, though; Alexander had long since begun looking beyond Darius, even beyond Persia. He was searching for fresh glory in the far eastern reaches of the old

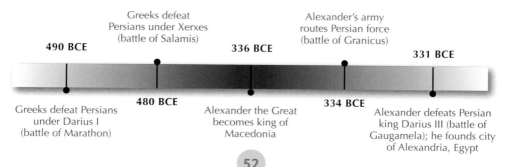

Greeks defeat Persians under Xerxes (battle of Salamis)

490 BCE

336 BCE

Alexander's army routes Persian force (battle of Granicus)

331 BCE

Greeks defeat Persians under Darius I (battle of Marathon)

480 BCE

Alexander the Great becomes king of Macedonia

334 BCE

Alexander defeats Persian king Darius III (battle of Gaugamela); he founds city of Alexandria, Egypt

Alexander's army crosses the Euphrates. Alexander conquered many places but never stayed very long. His army was always on the move.

empire. Parthia, Bactria, Carmania, Arachosia, and Sogdiana all fell to him. Conquering as he went, Alexander drove relentlessly to the east, toward India. He wanted to plunge straight into the subcontinent, but he was restrained by a few costly battles with Indian princes and by the demands of his soldiers. They had been away from Greece and Macedonia for a long time, and they were desperate to go home. Alexander had little choice but to agree. Marching down the Indus River, Alexander plot-

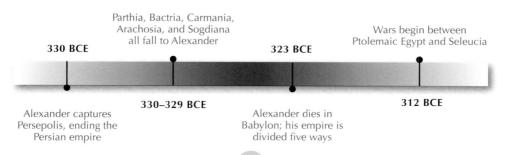

**330 BCE**

Parthia, Bactria, Carmania, Arachosia, and Sogdiana all fall to Alexander

**323 BCE**

Wars begin between Ptolemaic Egypt and Seleucia

Alexander captures Persepolis, ending the Persian empire

**330–329 BCE**

Alexander dies in Babylon; his empire is divided five ways

**312 BCE**

ted a course for Greece that would take him through Mesopotamia. It was there, in the city of Babylon, that he died of infection and fever in 323 BCE. He was only thirty-three years old.

Alexander had claimed a huge tract of land before his death. Lacking an acceptable heir, he left all of it to his five best generals, a group of men known as the Diadochi (dy-AD-uh-kee), meaning "successors." Three of them took control of Greece, Macedon, and what would someday become western Turkey. Two other generals, Seleucus (sih-LOO-kus) and Ptolemy (TAH-luh-mee), divided Egypt and the old Persian home territories between themselves. Seleucus received the largest chunk of land, encompassing Mesopotamia and the eastern portion of the fallen Persia. Ptolemy won the real prize. He got the legendary home of the pharaohs, with all its wealth and fields full of grain.

Although the division of Alexander's estate may seem a bit unfair to modern eyes, all of the parties involved at the time appeared to feel satisfied. But that feeling didn't last long. Each general-turned-king soon became envious of the others, and fighting broke out. Greece, Macedon, and what was known then

Alexander is shown the body of the slain Darius III. When he was told of Darius III's murder in Bactria, he was said to have mourned the Persian king's death. Alexander always had respect for other rulers.

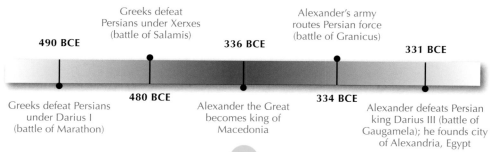

Greeks defeat
Persians under Xerxes
(battle of Salamis)

**490 BCE**

**336 BCE**

Alexander's army
routes Persian force
(battle of Granicus)

**331 BCE**

**480 BCE**

**334 BCE**

Greeks defeat Persians
under Darius I
(battle of Marathon)

Alexander the Great
becomes king of
Macedonia

Alexander defeats Persian
king Darius III (battle of
Gaugamela); he founds city
of Alexandria, Egypt

as Asia (western and central Turkey) experienced repeated bouts of warfare and constant political turmoil. These conflicts were often bitter and bloody, but they did not come anywhere close to matching the rivalry between the Seleucid (sih-LOO-kid) Empire and Ptolemaic (tah-luh-MAY-ik) Egypt. The kings of both places considered their realms to be "spear won,"[3] meaning that no one could challenge their authority or their territorial claims. Wars raged between these two giants for more

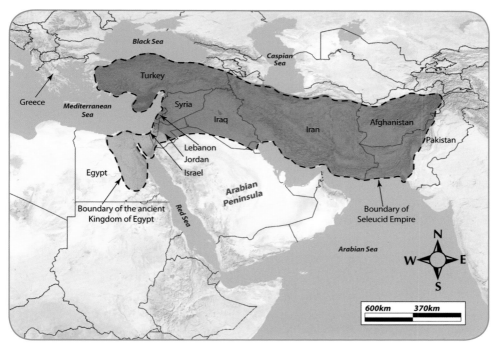

Most of the nations in the Middle East and part of Pakistan were once ruled by the Ptolemaic and Seleucid kingdoms. Only the states of the Arabian Peninsula never knew their rule.

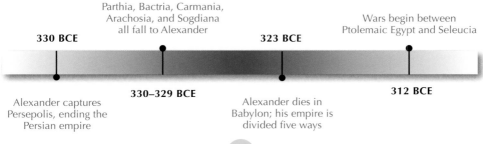

than a century. When not actually engaged in open hostilities, the Seleucids and Ptolemies were plotting for their next battle.

One point of fierce contention was the coastal strip between Anatolia and Egypt. This strip formed a buffer zone between Egypt and the Seleucid lands. Yet it also tempted both sides with its riches and resources. Trade was the crucial element in each case. The power that controlled the coastal cities controlled much of the trade in the ancient world. In time, the Seleucids gained a hold over the longest stretch of coastline, but their possessions were never completely safe. Ptolemaic Egyptians routinely raided Seleucid territory and occasionally struck off a city or town

Ptolemy I is portrayed entering Jerusalem in this medieval European drawing. Notice how the artist took ancient characters and put them in a medieval setting, dressing and living like people of that time.

and claimed it as their own. To make matters worse, the Seleucids got into the habit of constantly trying to expand their borders. The very process of taking over new places was tiring, and the burdens of governing far-flung, remote provinces proved to be too much in the end.

By the year 200 BCE, the Seleucids were exhausted and dangerously weakened. This condition invited challenges to their rule. The most serious of these came from a group of people from the northern mountain regions. They were the Parthians. This contestant's struggle with the Seleucids came just as the Ptolemaic Egyptians, weary as well from more than a century of conflict, were taking notice of an aggressive upstart city in Italy by the name of Rome. A new and violent chapter in the history of an ancient land was about to open.

## Ptolemies in Power

Ptolemaic Egypt not only outlasted the Seleucid Empire, it also surpassed the Seleucids in terms of its achievements. The Ptolemaic Egyptians had a strong army, of course, but they really shined in areas such as politics, art, and science. When Alexander's general, Ptolemy, took control of Egypt, he was a foreigner in a strange land. He was Macedonian, not Egyptian, and knew little about his new kingdom. Still, he knew that he had to govern well and keep the peace if he were to maintain his throne. So Ptolemy established a tradition of ruling the Egyptians gently and trying to fit into their society and culture. Although the Ptolemies—Ptolemy and his successors—looked down

A nineteenth-century engraving of Ptolemy I, called Soter (savior). The artist shows him wearing nineteenth-century clothes, but Ptolemy was known to have worn the fashions of the Egyptians. The crocodile symbolizes the Egyptian crocodile god Sobek, to whom Ptolemy built a temple.

on the Egyptian way of life and rarely ventured outside their capital of Alexandria, they quickly adopted Egyptian customs and traditions in order to make the people happy. They even went so far as to dress like, and call themselves, pharaohs, in the hopes of seeming more Egyptian.

The tactic worked. By and large, their Egyptian subjects accepted their Macedonian rulers. By acting as if they were not truly foreign conquerors, the Macedonians created an attachment between themselves and the native Egyptians that might otherwise never have existed.

Yet politics was merely one area in which the Ptolemies succeeded in strengthening their own position and enhancing the society and culture of Egypt. In fact, their time was one of great achievement for their adopted land and people. The arts flourished during their reign. Learning and scholarship were encouraged. Alexandria's huge library drew readers from all over the Mediterranean region; it housed perhaps over a million scrolls, the ancient equivalent of books. Egypt became renowned for its great philosophers, mathematicians, scientists, and astronomers.

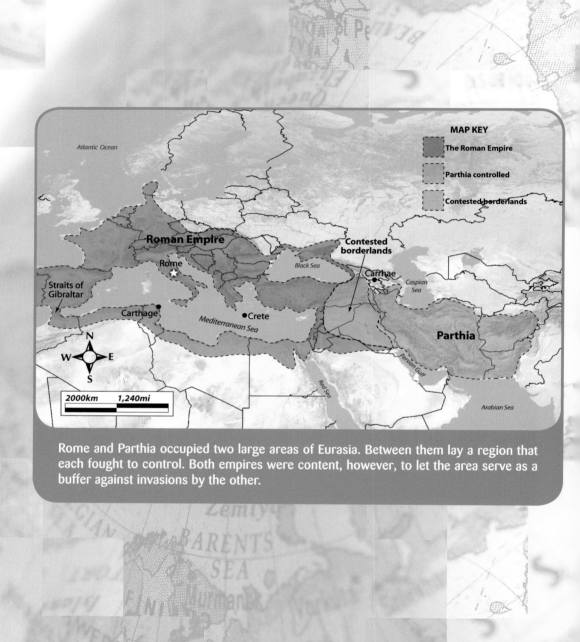

Rome and Parthia occupied two large areas of Eurasia. Between them lay a region that each fought to control. Both empires were content, however, to let the area serve as a buffer against invasions by the other.

# Chapter 6

## The Borderland of Empire

By the first century BCE, the Parthians had replaced the Seleucids as the overlords of the long-dead Persian Empire. Egypt was fast becoming a satellite in orbit around Rome. It would only be a short time before the Seleucid kingdom and Ptolemaic Egypt disappeared from the map, becoming yet more ancient places lost in time. This fact did not translate into peace and tranquillity, however. The script which had been in existence since the days of Akkad and Babylon stayed the same. Only the actors changed. Old conflicts over land and the domination of peoples would go on, with new contenders who would fight them out.

Parthia first appeared as a replacement for the Seleucid Empire around 250 BCE. Originally an eastern Persian province, Parthia began its rise to power in a series of rebellions. These local uprisings grew in scale and intensity over a period of some decades, and evolved into full-scale revolt against the Seleucids. Slowly but steadily, the Parthians chewed away at the empire. By 100 BCE, they had assumed control of everything east of the Euphrates, leaving Seleucid rule confined to the coastal region. Even here the Parthians continued to pressure their former masters.

The obvious vulnerability of the Seleucids not only encouraged the Parthians but also drew the attention of Rome. The Romans had been itching to expand to the east ever since they conquered Greece in 146 BCE. Taking what was left of the Seleucid Empire up to the borders of Egypt would put the Romans one step closer to their goal of making the Mediterranean Sea a Roman lake. Rome, which began its existence as a dusty village on the Tiber River, had already taken control of the western Mediterranean. Spain and North Africa became Roman territory after

People in the ancient Middle East lived life as best they could. In Turkey, for example, residents of the place once called Cappadocia carved the homes out of the mountains. These cave-homes have survived to modern times.

Rome defeated its chief western rival, Carthage, in a trio of bloody wars in the third and second centuries BCE. The victory allowed Rome to dominate trade and shipping from Crete to the Straits of Gibraltar.

Now the eastern waters became the target. Recognizing the obvious threat posed by Rome, Parthia signed a treaty with it in 92 BCE. The two powers agreed to call the Euphrates River the border between Parthian

c. 250 BCE — Romans conquer Greece

117 BCE

Parthians control everything east of the Euphrates

92 BCE

Parthia, a Persian province, begins its expansion

146 BCE

Rome briefly occupies Parthian Mesopotamia

100 BCE

Parthia and Rome sign a peace treaty

and Roman territory. While protecting Parthia, the settlement doomed the Seleucids. In a series of military campaigns, a Roman army overran the last remnant of the Seleucid Empire in Syria in 64 BCE. Places that today are found only in history books—Pergamum, Pontus, Bithynia, Cappadocia, and Cilicia—became Roman provinces.

Roman expansion into present-day Turkey completed the process of bringing Rome into direct contact and conflict with Parthia. Parthia, itself growing in size and influence, resented and feared the Roman presence in the Middle East. Their culture was totally different from that of Rome. While the Romans spoke Latin and drew their traditions from the farms and villages of Italy, the Parthians lived according to beliefs and practices that represented a blend of Greek and ancient Middle Eastern heritages. Roman and Parthian customs differed so much that each side regarded the other as utterly foreign. Rome and Parthia could not understand each other, and neither really cared to try.

The truce of 92 BCE was destined to be short-lived, and relations between Rome and Parthia soon became sour. The history of the ancient Middle East had already shown that war drove change in the region. So it was with these two powers. Representing two distinct worldviews, one fully Western, the other stubbornly Eastern with a heavy Greek accent, Rome and Parthia eventually came to blows. In fact, they fought one another fiercely for two centuries.

During those decades, the Parthians relentlessly attacked Roman border settlements. In retaliation, Roman armies twice invaded Parthian territory; both times they were defeated. In 53 BCE, the Roman general Marcus Licinius Crassus (MAR-kus lih-SIN-ee-us KRAS-us) fought a disastrous battle at Carrhae (KAR-ee). Having invaded Parthia with high hopes, Crassus's force was crushed by an army of Parthian horse archers. It was said that the Parthian attack at Carrhae sounded "like the roaring of wild

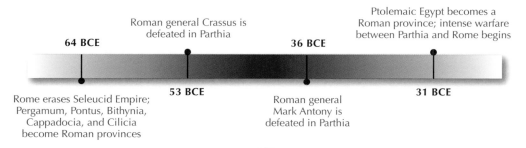

Roman general Crassus is defeated in Parthia

Ptolemaic Egypt becomes a Roman province; intense warfare between Parthia and Rome begins

64 BCE

36 BCE

53 BCE

31 BCE

Rome erases Seleucid Empire; Pergamum, Pontus, Bithynia, Cappadocia, and Cilicia become Roman provinces

Roman general Mark Antony is defeated in Parthia

Marcus Licinius Crassus rarely took advice. Despite dire warnings not to invade Parthia, Crassus was certain that he could gain a magnificent victory there.

predators, but intermingled with the sharpness of a thunderclap."[1] The general himself was captured and beheaded.

Seventeen years later, Marcus Antonius (or Mark Antony, as he is usually known) led another Roman contingent into Parthia. He was defeated as well. Only in 117 CE did a Roman army gain victory over the Parthians. The emperor Trajan (TRAY-jun) succeeded in taking Mesopotamia

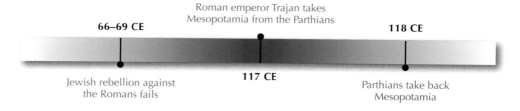

66–69 CE

Jewish rebellion against
the Romans fails

Roman emperor Trajan takes
Mesopotamia from the Parthians

117 CE

118 CE

Parthians take back
Mesopotamia

after a hard-fought campaign, but he could not hold it. Parthia regained the old imperial heartland a year later. By that time, with two hundred years of war behind them, it became clear that neither Rome nor Parthia would decisively win the shoving match in the Middle East.

Only part of the explanation for this stalemate had to do with military strategy and tactics. Both Rome and Parthia had other problems weighing on them. The Romans had to contend with challenges on other sections of its long frontier with the rest of the world. Barbarians were constantly pressing in on Roman territory and causing trouble. Worse yet, serious rebellions broke out in border provinces every so often. Perhaps the most memorable of these took place in 66 CE in Judea, the land that would someday be shared by Israelis and Palestinians. Jewish rebels rose up against Roman rule, waging an unsuccessful three-year war for independence.

Judea was also the place where the greatest social and cultural assault on Rome originated. The Romans were used to facing armed enemies on the field of battle, but this new challenger was spiritual. It was Christianity, and it fought with words rather than swords. The new religion developed a set of beliefs and values that went against everything Rome stood for. Christianity, with its message of love, equality, and heavenly authority, in time became a more dangerous foe than Parthia had ever been.

Parthia escaped the challenge of a new religion, but it had to face the same problems that had bedeviled every power that had tried to govern the Middle East. From the Akkadians to the Seleucids, empires and kingdoms in the region had struggled in vain to hold together places that were simply too large and too diverse. Parthia was no different. It could not keep its multiethnic, multicultural realm from disintegrating.

By the end of the first century CE, parts of the Parthian empire were beginning to drift away. In truth, Parthian rule had always been relatively

The Roman Empire is split in half; the Eastern (Byzantine) Empire wars with Sassanids

226 CE

476 CE

395 CE

Iranian king Ardashir defeats the Parthians; Sassanid Persia becomes imperial power

The Western Roman Empire collapses; area is ruled by Odoacer, a Hun

weak. Like the Assyrians and Persians before them, the Parthians figured that they could cheat history by governing the Middle East with a light hand. They allowed most of their vast domain to administer itself in the hopes that people would accept self-rule under Parthian overlords. The strategy ultimately failed. Although places like Bactria and Mesopotamia followed Parthian orders, they did so only when it suited their interests. Other provinces did what they were told only so long as Parthia remained militarily strong. The incessant wars with Rome took care of that.

As Parthia grew exhausted from war and the burdens of running a fragmented empire, places it had dominated began to break

The Roman emperor Trajan was one of the few rulers after Augustus who could manage Rome effectively. Under his hand, Rome prospered and won many military victories, especially against Parthia.

off and go their own way. It was only a matter of time before one of these peoples took it upon themselves to give ruling the Middle East a try. In 226 CE, an Iranian king named Ardashir (AR-duh-shur) confronted the Parthians and defeated them. Believing himself to be a descendant of the Achaemenids, he proclaimed a new Persian kingdom that would be known as the Sassanid (suh-SAH-nid) Empire. Parthia disappeared.

Roman emperor Trajan takes Mesopotamia from the Parthians

66–69 CE

118 CE

117 CE

Jewish rebellion against the Romans fails

Parthians take back Mesopotamia

Rome declined under the weight of global power as well. Invasions and migrations from almost every direction repopulated most of Europe with people who felt little if any loyalty to Rome. Every year, it seemed, the recently arrived immigrants became more difficult to assimilate and control. Occasional border attacks swelled into successive waves of invasion. Economic decline and social decay only made things worse. Romans, it seemed, had forgotten the advice of their first emperor, Augustus, who once warned them "to be satisfied with their present possessions and

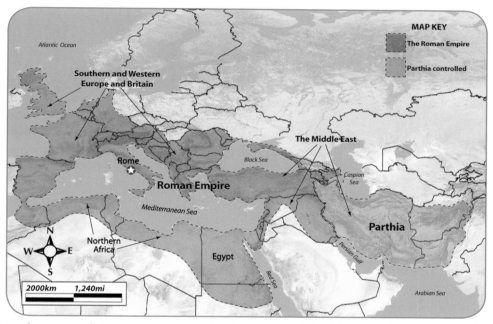

Modern areas that were once controlled by Rome and Parthia. Rome had indeed made the Mediterranean Sea a Roman lake.

The Roman Empire is split in half; the Eastern (Byzantine) Empire wars with Sassanids

226 CE

476 CE

395 CE

Iranian king Ardashir defeats the Parthians; Sassanid Persia becomes imperial power

The Western Roman Empire collapses; area is ruled by Odoacer, a Hun under no conditions to increase the empire. . . ."² "It would be hard to guard," Augustus continued, "and this would lead to danger of their losing what was already theirs."³ And so it was.

Under intense pressure, the Roman government reorganized itself and the empire split in two at the end of the fourth century CE. The Romans believed that it might be easier to defend themselves that way. There were now two Roman Empires, one Eastern and the other Western. This division didn't prevent the fall of the western half. In 410, a Visigoth (VIH-suh-goth) army stormed into the city of Rome and sacked it. An army of Vandals, another group of barbarian invaders, did the same in 455. The last West-

Led by King Ardashir I in 226 CE, the Iranians replaced the Parthians as the masters of the Middle East. Ardashir created a new Sassanid Persian empire.

ern Roman emperor stepped down in 476. His replacement was neither Roman nor even Italian. The new king of the Italian Peninsula was Odoacer (oh-doh-AY-sur). He was a Hun, a member of a tribe that originated in Asia and had only recently arrived in Europe.

The Western Empire was gone, but the Eastern one survived. It became known as the Byzantine (BIH-zun-teen) Empire, and its conflict with the new Sassanid Empire would be in many respects a replay of the previous one between Rome and Parthia. Once more, great rulers would try to succeed where so many others had failed. Each would attempt to make his land the ancient Middle East's sole superpower.

## The Battle of Carrhae

Marcus Licinius Crassus was perhaps the wealthiest man in ancient Rome. He was also an experienced military officer. Crassus was certainly no fool, but in 53 BCE he made a very foolish mistake. It was, in fact, a fatal mistake. In that year, Crassus decided to impress the people of Rome and further his political career by leading an invasion of Parthia.

The battle of Carrhae was a disaster for Rome. It would not be matched as a defeat in the history of Roman warfare until three legions were annihilated in the forests of Germany in the year 9 CE.

By then, Crassus had endured seven years in an uneasy alliance with Rome's legendary politicians—Pompey the Great and Julius Caesar. Working together in an arrangement known as the Triumvirate, the three men effectively ruled Rome. None of the men in the Triumvirate trusted the others very much, but Crassus felt especially suspicious. He was convinced that Pompey and Caesar wanted to cut him out of their deal. They, not he, had armies of loyal followers; Pompey and Caesar were popular among average Romans. Crassus had to find a way to improve his public image. A military victory in the East would do this nicely.

Crassus unwisely chose Parthia as his target. If he could defeat Rome's competitor in the Middle East, he imagined that he would become famous. Unfortunately for Crassus, the military campaign he launched ended in total disaster. Crassus's army was mauled by the Parthians at a place called Carrhae, in modern Syria. Crassus had expected an easy victory when he arrived in the East, and it seemed he would have it when only a small number of Parthian soldiers stood before him at Carrhae.

But the single line of Parthian infantry hid a much larger contingent of cavalry. When the Roman general attacked, the Parthian foot soldiers moved out of the way, allowing the horsemen to charge down upon their enemies. Simultaneously, another hidden cavalry force slammed into the Roman rearguard. During the battle, Crassus lost his legionary standards. These were banners mounted on poles and represented the fighting ability of the Roman soldiers. No other Roman general had ever suffered the loss of these standards.

Hoping to salvage a victory by talking rather than fighting, Crassus accepted a Parthian offer of a truce to discuss terms for peace. At the ensuing conference, Crassus was murdered. After killing Crassus, the Parthian king ordered his opponent's head cut off and sent it to be used as a prop in a theater performance.

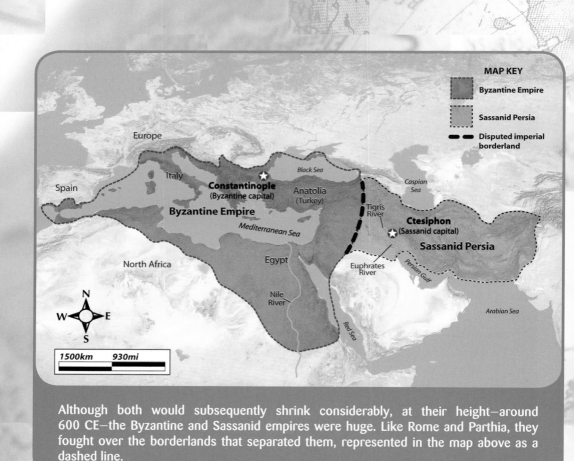

MAP KEY

▨ Byzantine Empire

▢ Sassanid Persia

●●● Disputed imperial borderland

Europe

Spain

Italy

Constantinople
(Byzantine capital)

Black Sea

Caspian Sea

Byzantine Empire

Anatolia
(Turkey)

Tigris River

Ctesiphon
(Sassanid capital)

Mediterranean Sea

Sassanid Persia

North Africa

Egypt

Euphrates River

Persian Gulf

Nile River

N
W ✦ E
S

Red Sea

Arabian Sea

1500km     930mi

Although both would subsequently shrink considerably, at their height—around 600 CE—the Byzantine and Sassanid empires were huge. Like Rome and Parthia, they fought over the borderlands that separated them, represented in the map above as a dashed line.

# Chapter 7

## East vs. West

Rome and Parthia faded into history, but new players carried on their contest for the ancient Middle East. After the fall of Rome, Sassanid Persia and the Byzantine Empire fought for another two centuries. The prize they wrestled for was power over a territory that stretched from the Tigris and Euphrates rivers to the sandy shores of the Mediterranean Sea. This space had once been ruled by the kings of Babylon, Assyria, and Achaemenid Persia. Like those monarchs, the crowned heads of Sassanid Persia and Byzantium concentrated their energies there.

Neither showed much interest in the area that is today known as South Asia; what would become Afghanistan, Pakistan, and eastern Iran pretty much went their own way. Nor did the Byzantines and the Sassanids take notice of the Arabian Peninsula. It was a bleak and barren desert dotted with oases and peopled by Arab nomads. There was nothing there to covet, so the two great empires mostly ignored Arabia. As things would turn out, both committed a costly error in doing so.

The Sassanids, just like their Achaemenid predecessors, were Iranians. They built their empire on a solidly Iranian foundation. The Sassanid king, in fact, referred to himself as "king of kings of the Iranians . . . the race of gods."[1] Culturally, politically, and geographically, the new Persia was centered on the southern provinces of the defunct Parthian state. The Sassanid capital, Ctesiphon (TEH-suh-fon), however, sat on the Tigris River not far from the older cities of Babylon and Seleucia, the old capital of the Seleucid Empire.

Like the Parthians before them, the Sassanids hoped to unite the Middle East under their rule, but they chose not to use Greek culture to do it.

All ancient cities and most large towns were heavily fortified by walls such as these. The Sassanids, continually under the threat of Byzantine invasion, became skilled at constructing city walls that kept attackers out while allowing the defenders to launch weapons from protected positions higher up.

The Parthians had kept much of the Greek legacy left by Alexander. The Sassanids, on the other hand, chose to stress local and regional customs over imported ones. They wanted their empire to seem more homegrown to its inhabitants, so that they might avoid the ethnic tension that plagued earlier efforts to stitch the region together. The Sassanids sought to avoid fragmentation by emphasizing diversity.

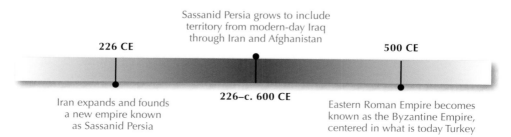

Sassanid Persia grows to include territory from modern-day Iraq through Iran and Afghanistan

226 CE

500 CE

Iran expands and founds a new empire known as Sassanid Persia

226–c. 600 CE

Eastern Roman Empire becomes known as the Byzantine Empire, centered in what is today Turkey

Little remains of Ctesiphon, the Sassanid capital. The vaulted hall that does still stand reveals the sophistication and beauty of its architecture.

Their plan worked at first. Moving outward from Iran and Iraq, the Sassanids expanded their territory and absorbed new peoples who accepted Persian rule. But they gained too much too quickly. Sassanid expansion to the west brought the new Persia into direct contact with the Byzantines, who jealously guarded their borders. All along this frontier, groups with little loyalty to Ctesiphon came under Persian command.

Far from strengthening the empire, these people proved to be a burden and a weak link in the Persian defensive chain. To the east, Sassanid forces clashed with the desert nomads and northern mountain tribes of Central and South Asia. Conflicts of one form or another popped up no matter in which direction the Sassanids turned. Thus, by the end of the

**613 CE**

Sassanid Persians occupy
Jerusalem; all-out war with
the Byzantines begins

**622–627 CE**

Byzantines, under emperor
Heraclius, defeat Persians
under emperor Khusru

**614 CE**

**627 CE**

Sassanid armies invade
Byzantine territory
and capture Syria

Byzantine armies invade
Sassanid Empire,
attacking into Iran

fifth century, the Sassanids had a grasp on nearly all of the old Parthian Empire, but nowhere was it firm.

Just as the Sassanids were carving out their own empire, the Byzantines were assuming the imperial mantle left behind by Rome. Well organized and prosperous, the Eastern Empire had established its capital at Constantinople (kahn-stan-tin-OH-pull), the old Greek city of Byzantium (bih-ZAN-tee-um). Now on its own, the Byzantine Empire went to

An early twentieth-century photograph of the Byzantine capital, Constantinople, which was famous for its public buildings. Its many churches, in the background, became mosques when the Turks captured the city in 1453.

Sassanid Persia grows to include territory from modern-day Iraq through Iran and Afghanistan

**226 CE**

**500 CE**

**226–c. 600 CE**

Iran expands and founds a new empire known as Sassanid Persia

Eastern Roman Empire becomes known as the Byzantine Empire, centered in what is today Turkey

For centuries, the walls of Constantinople protected the Byzantines. The advent of gun-powder weapons, especially monstrous cannons, eventually made ramparts such as these obsolete.

work. It developed a large and very efficient bureaucracy that made everything run smoothly. This was a big help, because the Byzantine population was incredibly diverse. Its inhabitants represented a mix of cultures, languages, and racial groups mingling together from modern Turkey to Egypt. Even though Christianity was the official religion, many others existed in the empire and were openly tolerated. The people lived on farms, in towns, and in large cities, where they grew wealthy from trade with Asia.

All the various peoples and cultures of the Byzantine Empire were protected by a formidable army. One historian echoes the conclusions of

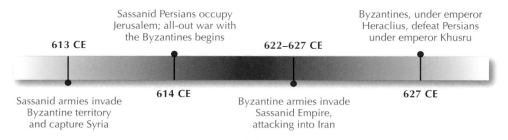

613 CE

Sassanid Persians occupy Jerusalem; all-out war with the Byzantines begins

622–627 CE

Byzantines, under emperor Heraclius, defeat Persians under emperor Khusru

614 CE

627 CE

Sassanid armies invade Byzantine territory and capture Syria

Byzantine armies invade Sassanid Empire, attacking into Iran

many others by noting that the Byzantine army was "the best in the world . . . man for man [it was] far superior to its opponents."[2] This was due in no small part to the Byzantine use of fully armored mounted troops. These metal-covered men outclassed other warriors of the time and became the model for the medieval knight.

Yet for all their strengths, the Byzantines had their weaknesses and faced many of the same problems confronting the Sassanids. The Byzantine emperors and the generals were forever on guard against barbarian invaders. The Byzantine frontier had to be constantly patrolled. Slavs, Bulgars, and other groups were always looking for ways to gain territory at the expense of their imperial neighbors. The empire also had to contend with the Sassanids. The borderline between the Byzantines and Sassanid Persians was a long one, running through the modern nations of Syria and Jordan almost to the Red Sea.

Heraclius celebrates the defense of Constantinople. His victories sealed the fate of Sassanid Persia. His defense of Constantinople and his conquest of Ctesiphon ended Sassanid dreams of continued glory.

Sassanid Persia grows to include territory from modern-day Iraq through Iran and Afghanistan

226 CE

500 CE

Iran expands and founds a new empire known as Sassanid Persia

226–c. 600 CE

Eastern Roman Empire becomes known as the Byzantine Empire, centered in what is today Turkey

While it marked out an area of cultural exchange and blending, it was also a battlefield.

Fighting between the Sassanids and the Romans, western and eastern, was nothing new. For over two hundred years, they had battled one another. The conflict only intensified after the Western Empire collapsed. The sixth century saw one Sassanid-Byzantine war after another. The climax came early in the seventh century. A particularly bitter war raged

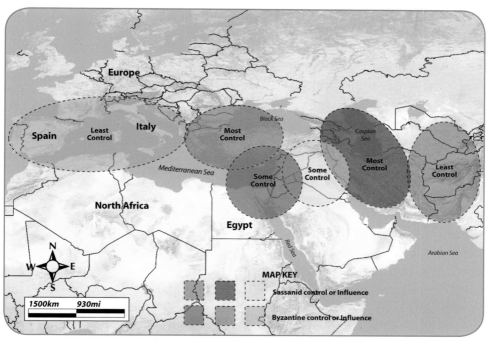

The extent of rule by the Byzantines and Sassanids in the areas they claimed. Empires, no matter how powerful, exercise varying degrees of control over their lands.

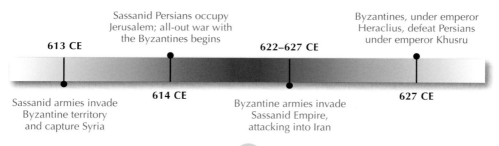

from 622 to 627, as the Byzantine and Sassanid armies tried to destroy each other. After the Persians failed at one point in an effort to take Constantinople, the tide of war turned against them. Led by the emperor Heraclius (her-AK-lee-us), the Byzantines slowly pushed their way through Turkey and down the Mediterranean coast. Next, they swung eastward and plunged into the Persian homeland. The forces of the Persian emperor Khusru (KUS-roo) fought valiantly, but they could not stop Heraclius's men. In 627, Khusru was deposed, and a new emperor made peace with the Byzantines. This essentially gave the invaders a complete victory.

Although purposely out of proportion, this medieval painting gives some idea as to how walled cities were attacked and defended. What is missing are representations of the catapults and other siege engines routinely used to weaken fortifications before an assault using scaling ladders like those in the foreground.

In reality, however, both sides lost. The long years of warfare left each empire exhausted. Their treasuries were empty, and their armies were tired. The Byzantines were in slightly better shape than the Sassanids, but neither side was as strong as it had been just a century earlier. Worse yet, their mutual fatigue came at a time when new threats to each side loomed ever larger. A wind was blowing off the deserts of Arabia, a wind that carried on its currents a new Middle Eastern power—Islam.

## The Byzantine Military

The Byzantine Empire represented the longest-lasting Christian presence in the history of the Middle East. From the year 395 until 1453, the Byzantines stood their ground against the Persians and later the Muslims. They survived in large part due to their superb army and navy, which only very slowly withered under the pressure of almost constant warfare.

The Byzantine army was a formidable opponent. It was a combined force, mixing infantry and cavalry into a single unit that always tried to attack first. The real core of the army was the cataphracts (KAT-uh-frakts), fully armored horsemen who used lances with unrivaled skill. Covered in chain mail and metal scales, the cataphracts rode armored horses that were big and fast. The individual cataphract was locked into his saddle by stirrups, an invention that made it virtually impossible to knock him off his mount. By locking his feet into the stirrups on either side of his horse, the cataphract had a way to keep his balance and, by pushing downward, resist the momentum of a blow that might move him sideways.

Byzantine infantrymen supported the cataphracts. They, too, were armored but more lightly. The infantry's primary weapons were the spear and sword. Infantry and cavalry alike were backed up by engineers and artillerymen, who operated complex war machines such as catapults, giant crossbows, and siege towers.

The army could rely upon the fine Byzantine navy for aid in tight situations. Byzantine ships were perhaps the best in the world. The same engineers who helped the soldiers on land also made sure that anyone attacking a Byzantine ship had to beware of an early sort of flamethrower which forced burning liquid, known as Greek fire, through a tube aimed at the enemy. Greek fire itself was a chemical mixture based on a highly flammable material called naphtha (NAF-thuh). Using this and other weapons, the Byzantine navy was strong enough not only to defend the capital city of Constantinople, but also to range out into the Mediterranean to protect the empire.

"Greek fire" was devastating but complicated and dangerous to use. The chemicals employed were both explosive and highly toxic. The sailors were occasionally poisoned or badly burned when the mixture ignited prematurely.

For Your Information

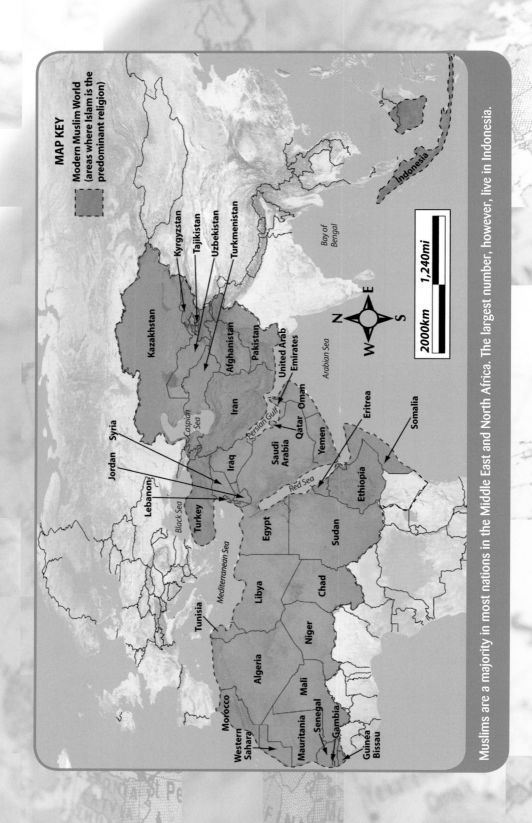

Muslims are a majority in most nations in the Middle East and North Africa. The largest number, however, live in Indonesia.

MAP KEY

Modern Muslim World
(areas where Islam is the
predominant religion)

Kazakhstan

Kyrgyzstan
Tajikistan
Uzbekistan
Turkmenistan

Afghanistan

Pakistan

Iran

United Arab
Emirates

Oman

Qatar

Syria

Jordan

Lebanon

Iraq

Saudi
Arabia

Yemen

Turkey

Eritrea

Somalia

Egypt

Ethiopia

Sudan

Libya

Chad

Tunisia

Niger

Algeria

Mali

Morocco

Mauritania

Senegal

Western
Sahara

Gambia

Guinea
Bissau

Indonesia

Bay of
Bengal

Arabian Sea

Persian Gulf

Red Sea

Black Sea

Caspian
Sea

Mediterranean Sea

N
W E
S

2000km

1,240mi

## Chapter 8

### Holy Warriors—An Islamic Middle East

Muhammad ibn Abdullah (moo-HAH-mid ibn ab-DOO-luh) grew up as an orphan. After his father died, his mother gave her baby boy up to a Bedouin (BED-oo-in) family who cared for him for a brief time. Muhammad then went back to his mother, but she died when Muhammad was six. He went to live with his grandfather. Muhammad's uncle took over after the grandfather's death two years later, and raised the boy as his own.

Muhammad's early life was not easy and seemed to promise only obscurity. The young Muhammad certainly had not the slightest idea that someday he would have, in the words of the scholar Karen Armstrong, "an experience that would ultimately change the history of the world."[1] Nor could Muhammad have guessed that, because of him, maps of the Middle East would be redrawn. The religion he would found, Islam, would create new places in time.

Born in Mecca in 570 CE, Muhammad lived an ordinary life, at least by Arabian standards. Arabs were accustomed to harshness and adversity, and orphans struggling to survive were nothing new. Like many others in his circumstances, Muhammad wanted a better life and worked hard to get it, eventually rising to become a merchant. He did his job well enough, but Muhammad really moved up in the world when he married a well-off older woman. Other Arab men might have been ashamed of taking such a wife, especially seeing how they would be dependent on her for financial support. This did not bother Muhammad, though. He loved his wife, Khadija (kah-DEE-juh), and was happy in his work. As a young man, Muhammad looked forward to a pleasant future.

In the year 610, everything suddenly changed. Muhammad had gone into the desert to reflect on his life. He stumbled home with incredible news. An angel had come to him, Muhammad told Khadija. The angel told him that he had been chosen to bring God's word to humanity. The heavenly figure, Muhammad claimed, had given him the job of telling the whole world about God's majesty and mercy. He was to be "the Lord's servant . . . His messenger."[2] From that point on, Muhammad announced to his wife, his work would be the work of Allah, the only true God.

Within a mere twenty-two years, this orphan built a new religion that would have a billion followers by the twenty-first century. However, Islam, which translates as "submission" (to the will of God), started off very small. In the beginning, its membership counted only Muhammad himself, Khadija, their servant, and Muhammad's cousin Ali (ah-LEE). But it grew quickly. Soon it became the dominant force in the politics, society, and culture of the Middle East. Islam became the foundation for an empire that covered the entire ancient Middle East, from the Mediterranean Sea to India. It reached as far north as Central Asia and as far south as the Sahara. For seven hundred years, it even had a foothold in Europe: a Muslim kingdom existed in Spain from the eighth century to the fifteenth century.

Yet, as so often in the past, the Muslim empire had to fight to hold itself together. It was plagued by difficulties, internal and external, similar to those faced by everyone else who had tried to unite the Middle East under a single power. Despite the dreams of Muhammad's early followers, the ancient problems of empire in the Middle East proved to be too much.

Islam's formative years spanned the period from 618 to 632. After expanding his early following, Muhammad set out to convert all of Arabia to his new faith. He ran into a good deal of opposition early on,

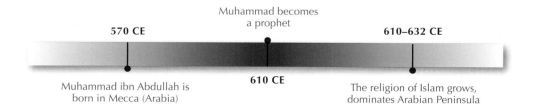

Muhammad becomes
a prophet

**570 CE**

**610–632 CE**

**610 CE**

Muhammad ibn Abdullah is
born in Mecca (Arabia)

The religion of Islam grows,
dominates Arabian Peninsula

especially after his well-respected uncle died and left Muhammad on his own. Some people in Mecca (MEH-kuh), the city where he lived, were frightened by Muhammad's message of charity, simplicity, and earnest prayer. Others resented his claim that God loved the poor and weak more than the rich and strong. For whatever reason, many Meccans wanted Muhammad to stop preaching; some even wanted him dead.

In 622, fearing for his life, Muhammad fled to the city of Yathrib (YAH-thrub, later named Medina), a journey Muslims remember as the Hegira

At least once in his or her lifetime, a Muslim must go to Mecca. The journey, known as the hajj, brings millions of devout worshipers to the holiest site in Islam, the Kaaba (the black stone structure in the upper right-hand corner).

Muhammad dies

630 CE

637 CE

632 CE

Muhammad's soldiers
capture Mecca

After conquering Palestine, Muslim
caliph Umar takes Sassanid Persia

The mosque of Masjid Nabawi is a center of Muslim worship in Medina, Islam's second city. Medina was home to the Prophet Muhammad during his exile from Mecca.

(hih-JY-ruh). Civil war followed. Battles, large and small, raged for eight years. At last, in 630, Muhammad's soldiers captured Mecca. Islam had won. The taking of Mecca signaled the political and geographic victory of a religion that, like Christianity and Judaism, worships one god, Allah, whose words are supposedly contained in the Muslim holy book, the Qur'an (kuh-RAHN). It was also a personal victory for the one-time

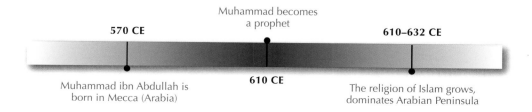

Muhammad becomes
a prophet

570 CE                                                                           610–632 CE

610 CE

Muhammad ibn Abdullah is
born in Mecca (Arabia)

The religion of Islam grows,
dominates Arabian Peninsula

orphan boy who grew up to be the Prophet. Two years after his astonishing triumph capped his life's work, Muhammad died.

Many religions break up after their founders die, but Islam became stronger. Muhammad had united the Arabs as no one had ever done. "Every Muslim is a brother to every other Muslim," he said in his last sermon to his people, "you are now one brotherhood."[3] Muhammad's successors carried his faith to even greater victories than the Prophet himself had achieved. Abu Bakr (uh-BOO BAW-kurr), the Muslim leader, or caliph, from 632 to 634, completed the process of spreading Islam to every corner of Arabia. The caliph Umar (OO-mahr), who ruled from 634 to 644, conquered Palestine and the city of Jerusalem. He then stormed into Sassanid Persia. Exhausted by the Byzantine wars, the Sassanids were no match for the determined Muslim invaders. The Sassanid capital fell in 637. Once more, Persia was erased from the map.

From there, the religion of Muhammad spread across North Africa, but not before the Muslim community dissolved into civil war again. Uthman (ooth-MAHN), who succeeded Umar, ruled from 644 to 656, a time of indecision and turmoil. Muslims disagreed about the future direction their religion should take. The result was a three-way contest between Uthman's followers and those of Muhammad's last wife, Aisha (AH-ee-shah), and the Prophet's cousin and son-in-law, Ali. Years of fierce combat and the assassination of Ali culminated in a split in Islam. Muslims loyal to Ali called themselves Shia; the rest became known as Sunni. The division endures to this day.

After the civil war, Islam's expansion resumed. By the early eighth century, Muslim armies had pushed to the gates of Constantinople in the east and to the Pyrenees (PEER-uh-neez) Mountains in the west. Defeats outside Constantinople (718) and at the battle of Tours in France (732) kept the Muslims from conquering Europe but did not prevent further

630 CE

Muhammad's soldiers
capture Mecca

Muhammad dies

632 CE

637 CE

After conquering Palestine, Muslim
caliph Umar takes Sassanid Persia

Muslim gains. In time, a stalemate developed. The Muslims could not beat the Christian Europeans, yet the Christians were unable to destroy Islam.

Eyeing one another with fear and suspicion, the two groups grew increasingly hostile toward each other. Neither side could score a military victory over the other, so their warfare shifted into the area of trade. Each sought to control access to the lucrative trade routes to China and India and deny it to their opponent. The Middle East had long been a crossroads between the West and Asia. The Muslims wanted to use their position between Asian supply and European demand as a weapon in their struggle against the Europeans. Through taxation and tariffs, Muslim rulers hoped to grow rich from the trade that flowed along the roads to the East, such as the well-traveled Silk Road. They also hoped to dominate the West through economic means.

Trade was a relatively peaceful and bloodless battlefield. Muslims and Christian Europeans might argue and jostle for economic advantage, but no one died. The situation became very different in the Holy Land. Palestine, in particular Jerusalem, was sacred to Christians, Muslims, and Jews alike. Jews believed that the Holy Land had been promised to them through Moses. Christians knew it as the birthplace of Jesus. Muslims learned as children that Muhammad had gone to Jerusalem before going up into heaven. Each religion, reading its own stories, claimed the area that today contains the nation of Israel, the Palestinian Authority, and parts of Syria and Jordan. Only the Christians and Muslims, however, possessed the military might to force the issue.

Over the centuries, Christian resentment of Islam possession of the Holy Land grew. They did not particularly mind if people in places like Mesopotamia and Persia lived under the crescent-moon banner of Islam, but the Holy Land was a different matter. Jesus had been born there, and

The Muslims split into Shia
and Sunni factions

637 CE

680–1000 CE

680 CE

Sassanid capital, Ctesiphon,
captured by Arabs; Arab
capital built at Baghdad

Muslim expansion continues,
creating Islamic empire

The Silk Road was really a series of dusty trails winding their way from China to the Middle East. The land was unforgiving, and travelers were advised to be careful.

he died on the cross there. It was the place where Jesus had preached about love and the kingdom of God.

The Christian attempt to break the Muslim hold over the Holy Land became known as the Crusades, a series of religious wars fought between the eleventh and thirteenth centuries. Actually, the Crusaders' aims went beyond simple reconquest. Their overall objective included both the destruction of Muslim power and the ending of Byzantine authority in the East. The Europeans hoped that the Byzantines were so weak after

680–1000 CE

European Christian Crusaders invade the Middle East eight times

1274 CE

Islam takes root in Spain

1095–1274 CE

Muslims retain control of Middle East, but their hold is weak

Jerusalem contains sites sacred to Muslims, Jews, and Christians. The Dome of the Rock (left), where Muhammad is believed to have ascended into heaven, is located directly atop the ruins of the biblical Temple of Solomon, the walls of which are still visible.

fighting the Sassanids and then the Arab Muslims that they could be forcibly reunited with the West. Some Europeans actually imagined that something like the old Roman Empire could be revived as a new Christian empire that would extend its rule into the Middle East.

Eight times, European Crusaders invaded the Middle East. During the First Crusade, Christian armies conquered Jerusalem, only to lose it in the course of the Third Crusade nearly a century later. The Fourth Crusade saw Western Christians slaughtering their Eastern brethren as a Crusader army attacked and ravaged Constantinople.

637 CE

The Muslims split into Shia and Sunni factions

680–1000 CE

Sassanid capital, Ctesiphon, captured by Arabs; Arab capital built at Baghdad

680 CE

Muslim expansion continues, creating Islamic empire

# Holy Warriors—An Islamic Middle East

For two hundred years, the wars between Christians and Muslims tore at the Middle East. As had happened since the days of Akkad, great powers fought to control ancient places. And as in the past, the contestants eventually weakened themselves to the point where new players came onto the stage. Europe abandoned its Middle Eastern ambitions in the mid-thirteenth century, leaving their Muslim opponents in control of the region.

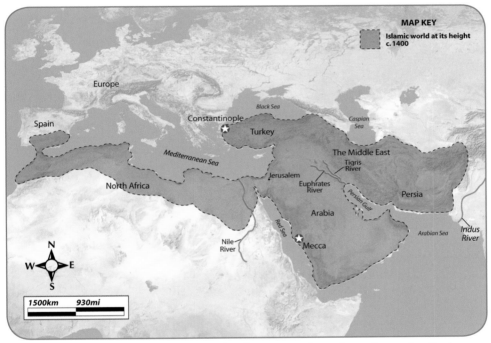

Muslim warriors and bureaucrats united a diverse number of peoples under the banner of Islam. By the fifteenth century, Islam was the dominant religion from the Mediterranean shores of Spain to the Indus River.

European Christian Crusaders
invade the Middle East eight times

680–1000 CE          1274 CE

1095–1274 CE

Islam takes root in Spain          Muslims retain control of Middle
East, but their hold is weak

The Fourth Crusade was a catastrophe for the residents of Constantinople. Although governed by Arab Muslims, the citizens were Christians. They suffered greatly as fellow Christians sacked the city in 1204.

But this was far from total victory. The Arab Muslim system of government, based on caliphs supported by various local sultans, never recovered from the stress placed on it by the Crusades. The Muslim caliph Mu'awiyah (moo-AH-wee-ah) had once declared that he could hold the Muslim empire together with a hair. "Let a single hair bind me to my people," he famously boasted, "and I will not let it snap."[4] So he and his successors did, until the Crusades cut that connection. The era of Arab Muslim domination passed. Once again, a new force emerged out of the wreckage of war. As always, it set itself to succeed in trying to create a Middle Eastern empire where so many others had failed.

## Saladin—The Sultan of Islam

As the English King Richard I, the Lionheart, lay on his sickbed in Palestine in 1192 during the Third Crusade, he certainly did not expect that he would receive a get-well gift from one of the greatest military geniuses in the history of the Middle East. As the king's fever raged, Richard was presented with a refreshing bowl of fruit and snow, courtesy of his opponent—Saladin.

Saladin, whose full name was Salah al-Din Yusef ibn Ayyub, was that kind of soldier. Generous, honorable, and yet a fierce warrior, Saladin had grown up fighting for Islam. Born in 1137, he was the son of a Kurdish commander and politician. His father, Ayyub, had to flee Saladin's birthplace, Tikrit (tih-KREET), during a local political dispute. After

Richard I is the best remembered of the Crusader kings. His victories abroad, however, did not guarantee his reign at home in England. There he was eventually deposed by his own brother, King John I.

that, Ayyub entered into the service of a powerful Muslim leader and became an influential figure at court. The young Saladin thus grew up in a charged climate and learned quite early how to maneuver through complex corridors of twelfth-century Muslim politics. Saladin learned from his father how to manipulate the affairs of state to benefit himself.

Yet through his boyhood, Saladin also trained for war and discovered how to lead men into battle. His uncle was the teacher there. He taught Saladin how to wield a sword and lance and how to command troops. By the time he was a man, Saladin was ready for greatness and lasting fame. All he needed was a chance to prove himself. His opportunity materialized in 1173, when he assumed the role of sultan of Syria and Egypt after winning the civil war that followed the death of his predecessor. For the next twenty years, Saladin fought against Muslim rebels and Christian Crusaders alike. His most famous victory came in 1187. In that year, Saladin's armies recaptured the holy city of Jerusalem, which had been lost to the Christians nearly a century earlier. After bringing Richard and his Crusaders to a standstill on the battlefield in 1192, Saladin made a peace that guaranteed Muslim control of Jerusalem and the whole of the Middle East. Sadly for his people, the man who became known as the sultan of Islam, "the ornament and the admiration of the world,"[5] died a year later.

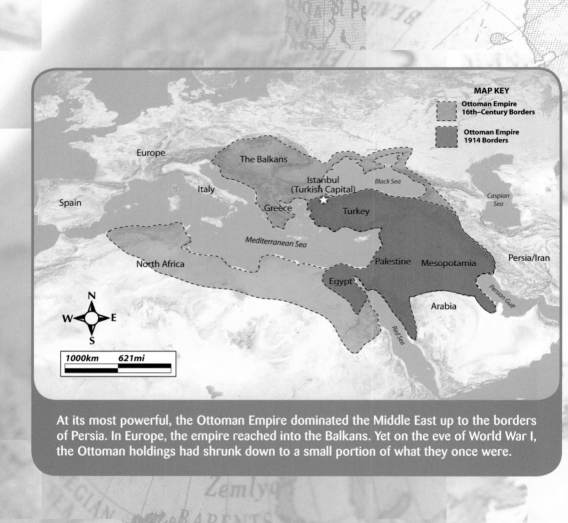

**MAP KEY**

Ottoman Empire
16th–Century Borders

Ottoman Empire
1914 Borders

Europe

The Balkans

Istanbul
(Turkish Capital)

Black Sea

Caspian
Sea

Italy

Spain

Greece

Turkey

Mediterranean Sea

North Africa

Palestine

Mesopotamia

Persia/Iran

Egypt

Persian Gulf

Red Sea

Arabia

N
W — E
S

1000km    621mi

At its most powerful, the Ottoman Empire dominated the Middle East up to the borders
of Persia. In Europe, the empire reached into the Balkans. Yet on the eve of World War I,
the Ottoman holdings had shrunk down to a small portion of what they once were.

# Chapter 9

## Allah's Empire—The Ottoman Turks

The victory over the European Christians should have brought the Muslims together in triumph. Instead, it resulted in disagreement and conflict. Islam broke apart after the Crusades. Local warlords and regional sultans quarreled among themselves and competed for power. Syria, the heartland of Saladin's sultanate, went its own way. So did the Muslim state of Rum (ROOM), which occupied a large part of modern Turkey. To the south, Egypt, under the rule of the Mamluks (MAAM-lukes), operated as an independent Muslim kingdom. Throughout the Middle East, Muslim unity disintegrated.

These divisions could not have come at a worse time. A new threat had appeared in the East. An army of Mongols, the conquerors of Central Asia, was moving westward, sweeping all before it. Led by Hulagu (hoo-LAH-goo), the grandson of Genghis Khan, the warlord who launched the Mongol invasions of Central and East Asia, the Mongols captured Baghdad in 1258 and seemed ready to roll all the way to the Mediterranean Sea. Their defeat by the Mamluks in 1260 prevented this, but the Mongols still controlled a wide swath of ground in the very center of the Muslim world.

Temporarily stopped, the Mongols settled down and their warlike days seemed over. Their descendants, however, soon picked up where the original conquerors had left off. By the end of the fourteenth century, their armies were on the move again. Led by Tamerlane (TAM-ur-layn), the invaders seized city after city and crushed one Muslim army after another. Tamerlane's brutality was legendary. Following the capture of one town, for example, he "ordered all those over fourteen years be

A statue of Tamerlane in Uzbekistan. The Mongols had a reputation for merciless violence. Their descendants under Tamerlane maintained that heritage. Some modern historians, however, argue that most of the tales of Tamerlane's brutality were exaggerated in order to intimidate his enemies.

beheaded . . . and with the heads he constructed a tower in the center of the city."[1] The same eyewitness reported that later Tamerlane massacred the children of another city by having them trampled to death by horses.

Riding out of his capital city of Samarkand (SAM-ur-kand), in modern-day Uzbekistan (ooz-BEK-ih-stan), Tamerlane conquered Iran and Mesopotamia. He took the ancient city of Babylon and, according to one observer, "burnt it. Then had the earth ploughed . . . so that nobody should know whether there had been houses or no."[2] From there, Tamerlane's army burst into Syria and finally into Anatolia, where in 1402 it defeated the forces of the Osmanli (oz-MAN-lee)—a Turkish tribe that became known to history as the Ottomans (AH-tuh-munz).

Almost one hundred years earlier, led by their chief, Osman (OZ-mun), the Turks had been just another wandering band of Muslim nomads and herders. The only thing that set them apart was the timing of their arrival in the Middle East, just

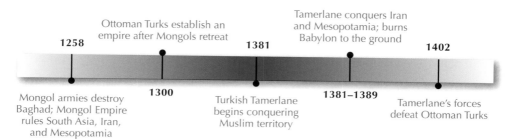

1258

Mongol armies destroy Baghad; Mongol Empire rules South Asia, Iran, and Mesopotamia

1300

Ottoman Turks establish an empire after Mongols retreat

1381

Turkish Tamerlane begins conquering Muslim territory

1381–1389

Tamerlane conquers Iran and Mesopotamia; burns Babylon to the ground

1402

Tamerlane's forces defeat Ottoman Turks

Samarkand was an important trading city. Whoever had possession of it could profit handsomely from the city's prime location on the East-West trade routes.

at the end of the Crusades. Taking advantage of the confusion that followed the last of the Christian invasions, the Ottomans established themselves in Anatolia. Over the course of the next century, they steadily gained more and more land. The Ottomans, in fact, were well on their way to building a powerful Muslim state when Tamerlane showed up. His defeat of the Ottoman army seemed to doom the Turks' hopes of glory.

However, the fearsome Tamerlane suddenly died in 1405. Released from the grip of their Central Asian masters, the Ottomans flourished once more. The Turkish rulers (or sultans, as they were called by their people) Mehmed I (meh-MET, 1413–1421) and Murad II (mur-AUD, 1421–1451) turned the Ottoman nation into a genuine empire. They consolidated Ottoman rule, set up a new bureaucracy, and expanded the army by

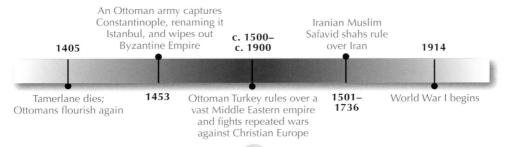

| 1405 | An Ottoman army captures Constantinople, renaming it Istanbul, and wipes out Byzantine Empire | c. 1500– c. 1900 | Iranian Muslim Safavid shahs rule over Iran | 1914 |

Tamerlane dies; Ottomans flourish again

1453

Ottoman Turkey rules over a vast Middle Eastern empire and fights repeated wars against Christian Europe

1501– 1736

World War I begins

recruiting large numbers of slaves who became elite troops known as janissaries (JAN-uh-sayr-eez). These were professional soldiers who were fiercely loyal to the sultan they served. All the while, the emerging Ottoman Empire continued to gnaw at the remains of the Byzantine homeland.

Byzantine influence and authority had been waning for centuries. By the mid-1400s, very little of it remained. Byzantine territory had shrunken to a parcel of land around the capital of Constantinople. The once-mighty Byzantine army was exhausted, and the emperors could no longer defend their people. Everyone knew that a final contest between the Byzantines and the Turks loomed and that the stakes would be high.

The battle for supremacy in the Middle East came when an Ottoman army arrived outside Constantinople in February 1453. For the next four months, the Turks laid siege to the Byzantine city. The sultan Mehmed II, with an army of 80,000 men and seventy huge cannons, was determined to wipe away the last remnants of the old Roman presence east of Greece. The Ottomans also wanted to ensure that Islam ruled as the region's dominant faith.

Given these goals, the Turks threw everything they had against the beleaguered Byzantines. Giant cannonballs pounded Constantinople's walls; Turkish engineers tried to dig tunnels under the ramparts to bring them crashing down. Several times, the Turks launched direct frontal attacks in an attempt to storm the city. At last, the Ottoman soldiers managed to fight their way over the walls using enormous ladders. Once inside, they fought hand-to-hand with the Byzantine troops. The Byzantine emperor himself joined in, only to be cut down by Turkish swords. As their army collapsed, the citizens of Constantinople screamed, "What is to become of us? . . . The Turks are slaughtering the Romans within the City's walls!"[3]

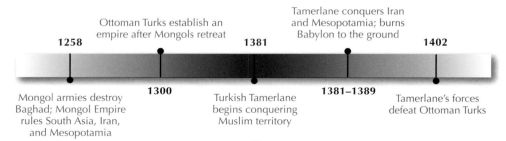

**Mehmed II entered Constantinople as a victorious Muslim hero. Europeans saw his triumph as the beginning of an enduring rivalry.**

Frantically, the people did all they could to stop the Ottomans. Nothing worked. On May 29, 1453, Constantinople fell. For the next three days, the Turks pillaged the city. In celebration, Mehmed II had the Byzantine emperor's head stuffed as a trophy.

Ottoman domination of the Middle East was now undisputed. The empire was free to grow and develop. Over the next 450 years, the Ottomans extended their rule southward through Palestine into Egypt. They grabbed North Africa as far as modern Tunisia. Ottoman armies pushed eastward into Mesopotamia and occupied that ancient land.

Only along the borders of Iran did they pause. While the Ottomans had been busy fighting the Byzantines, a native Iranian Muslim dynasty had arisen. From 1501 until 1736, Safavid (sah-FAH-weed) shahs ruled over Iran and made many lasting changes. The most important of these was the establishment of the Shia version of Islam as the exclusive Iranian religion.

The Safavids of Iran and the Ottomans fought continually. The Turks never did succeed in conquering the ancient heartland of Persia. Nor did

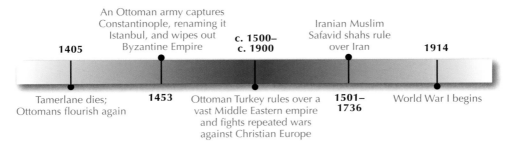

**1405**

**Tamerlane dies; Ottomans flourish again**

An Ottoman army captures Constantinople, renaming it Istanbul, and wipes out Byzantine Empire

**1453**

Ottoman Turkey rules over a vast Middle Eastern empire and fights repeated wars against Christian Europe

**c. 1500– c. 1900**

Iranian Muslim Safavid shahs rule over Iran

**1501– 1736**

**1914**

World War I begins

they ultimately come out on top in the bitter contest with the Europeans, though they did enjoy some successes. From the sixteenth through the nineteenth centuries, the Ottomans launched wars of conquest aimed at southeastern Europe and the Balkans. Greece and the modern states of Bosnia and Serbia, for example, became parts of the Ottoman Empire at different points in history. Turkish armies penetrated into Europe as far as Hungary and Austria. The Turkish fleet challenged the seafaring Italian cities for command of the Mediterranean trade routes. Yet despite these victories, each war the Ottomans conducted weakened the empire a little more. The Ottoman economy was never strong, and military operations drained off vital resources.

A Russian army enters Samarkand. The Russians were among the first Europeans since the Romans to attempt to rule over the Middle East. As always, local peoples resisted fiercely.

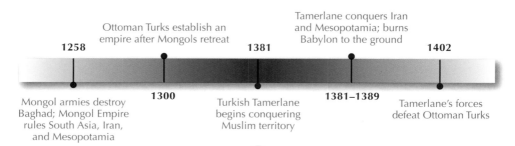

Ottoman Turks establish an empire after Mongols retreat

Tamerlane conquers Iran and Mesopotamia; burns Babylon to the ground

1258

1381

1402

1300

1381–1389

Mongol armies destroy Baghad; Mongol Empire rules South Asia, Iran, and Mesopotamia

Turkish Tamerlane begins conquering Muslim territory

Tamerlane's forces defeat Ottoman Turks

Worse still, the Ottomans wrestled with the old problem of running an empire made up of hundreds of different cultures, religions, and languages. Turkish rule was never secure and was resented everywhere it was carried. So when World War I broke out in 1914, the Ottoman Empire began to disintegrate. It was simply too large and too diverse to hold together under the weight of a massive global conflict. Rebellions swept over Ottoman territory, most violently among the Arabs. Arab warlords joined with the invading British armies to defeat the Ottoman forces. In 1918, Ottoman Turkey surrendered to the British and their French allies. Two years later, the victors stripped the Turks of all their territory except that in Turkey itself.

Like Babylon, Assyria, and Persia, the Ottoman Empire failed in its quest to unite and dominate the Middle East. No city, kingdom, or empire had ever been strong enough to do that. The many peoples and societies of the Middle East had defied them all. The Ottoman Empire, for all its glory and might, became just another place in time.

Today, its former lands comprise an array of states. The old Ottoman heartland is now the nation of Turkey, a vibrant and modern country. To its south lie Lebanon, Syria, Jordan, the Jewish state of Israel, and the much-contested areas of Palestine governed by the semi-autonomous Palestinian Authority.

Ancient Mesopotamia, once a prized possession of the Ottoman sultans, became Iraq soon after World War I. Although stable and prosperous for much of its history prior to independence, Iraq suffered under a military dictatorship whose leader, Saddam Hussein, had many political enemies. After the American invasion of 2003, Iraq slipped into political chaos and economic decline, and religious conflict between Iraqi Sunni and Shia escalated. The Arab lands that produced the great revolt of 1916 are today the oil-rich nations of the Arabian Peninsula, dominated by

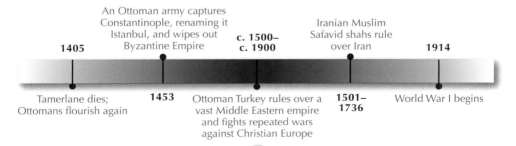

| | An Ottoman army captures Constantinople, renaming it Istanbul, and wipes out Byzantine Empire | c. 1500– c. 1900 | Iranian Muslim Safavid shahs rule over Iran | 1914 |

1405

Tamerlane dies; Ottomans flourish again | 1453 | Ottoman Turkey rules over a vast Middle Eastern empire and fights repeated wars against Christian Europe | 1501– 1736 | World War I begins

Saudi Arabia. Their combined wealth totals trillions of dollars, making this former desert wasteland perhaps the richest place on earth.

What used to be the core of the Persian Empire is now the Shia Muslim–dominated state of Iran. The eastern reaches of ancient Persia today are filled by Afghanistan and much of Pakistan. Assyria lies in northern Iraq; Babylonia is in the southern part of that war-torn country. The city-states of old Mesopotamia sit in one or another Iraqi province.

In every case, their names identify ruins rather than living cities. Sumer, Akkad, Babylon, and Nineveh once hummed with political and economic activity. From them came the orders and edicts of kings who

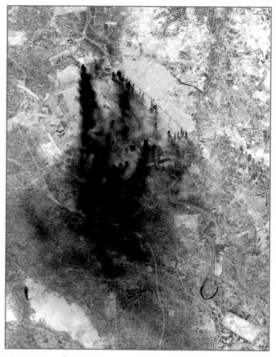

NASA Landsat 7 image of Baghdad, Iraq, April 2, 2003. The dark streaks are smoke from oil well fires set in an attempt to hinder attacking U.S. air forces. War has always plagued the Middle East, and little has changed over the centuries.

ruled the world in their day. In modern times, the capitals of Sumeria, Babylonia, and Assyria are marked on maps as archaeological sites, points of historical interest that no longer carry any other significance. Even the monumental Persian capital city of Persepolis, where ambassadors from throughout the Middle East and Mediterranean came to pay

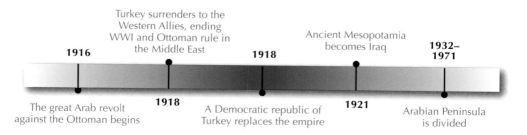

1916

Turkey surrenders to the Western Allies, ending WWI and Ottoman rule in the Middle East

1918

Ancient Mesopotamia becomes Iraq

1932–1971

The great Arab revolt against the Ottoman begins

1918

A Democratic republic of Turkey replaces the empire

1921

Arabian Peninsula is divided

tribute to the King of Kings, stands silent except for the snapping of tourist cameras and the sounds of archaeologists' shovels.

Likewise, the power and glory of ancient Egypt has faded away. The old centers of Egyptian culture and religion along the Nile River have become curiosities to be visited by foreigners and studied by scholars. The last vestiges of Ptolemaic Egyptian society have long since vanished, replaced by a thriving Muslim way of living and thinking.

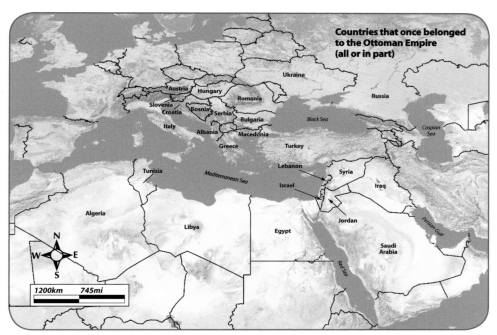

Few casual observers remember the Ottoman Empire, yet many modern states were once Ottoman provinces.

1935
Core of the ancient Persian Empire is officially renamed Iran

2003

The United States invades Iraq; its goal is to etablish a peaceful, democratic Middle East

2006
Iran and the United States vie for regional influence; once again, the West and what was Persia are in conflict

The U.N. imposes sanctions on Iran for developing nuclear technology

2007

The legacy of warfare can be seen in some of the architecture of the Middle East. Alexandria in Egypt, famous for its library, also possessed formidable defensive works such as the Citadel, above.

Alexandria, the city of Alexander the Great, remains a bustling population center, but most of what had been built by Alexander's engineers has crumbled. Much of the rest lies underwater in the modern harbor, inundated by the rising Mediterranean Sea. The young Macedonian king who defeated Darius III at Gaugamela likely would not recognize the city that bears his name. He probably would not recognize many of the other places that dot modern maps. The same could be said for the other rulers of a world that has disappeared in time.

## The Great Arab Revolt

During World War I, the Ottoman Turks faced an ancient problem. Like so many Middle Eastern empires before them, the Turks struggled to keep together a territory filled with diverse peoples and cultures. The Ottoman Empire in 1914 stretched from Mesopotamia to Egypt and from Arabia to Turkey. It was as large as any of its ancient counterparts and every bit as difficult to rule.

Shortly after Turkey went to war with Russia, Britain, and France, the Arabs, who had long resented Turkish rule, rose up against their masters. In June 1916, led by their own leaders, ably assisted by courageous British officers such as T.E. Lawrence ("Lawrence of Arabia"), Arab armies attacked the Turks in Arabia. Employing traditional hit-and-run tactics suited to desert warfare, the Arabs ham-

Lawrence of Arabia is recalled today as being a courageous soldier. He thought of himself, however, as a tireless advocate for the rights and independence of the people of the Middle East.

mered at the Turks. Turkish outposts were raided, supply depots were destroyed, rail and telegraph lines were cut. Although vastly outnumbered, the highly mobile Arab forces defeated the Turks at every turn.

By December 1916, the western shore of the Arabian Peninsula had been cleared of Turkish troops and an independent Arab kingdom was established there. Meanwhile, British soldiers unsuccessfully invaded Gaza (GAH-zah) early in 1917 in an effort to support their Arab allies. The Arabs responded by picking up the pace of their assault on the Ottomans. Giving operational command of their men to Lawrence, the Arab leaders threw an army against the Turkish fort at Aqaba (AH-kuh-bah) and captured it in July 1917.

From there the Arabs moved northward into Palestine, helping the British capture Gaza and take Jerusalem that December. Teaming up with the British again, the Arabs carried their revolt into Lebanon and Syria, seizing the cities of Beirut (bay-ROOT), Aleppo (uh-LEP-poe), and Damascus. By October 1918, the Ottomans and their empire were finished. One of history's great powers had been brought down, and the Arab Revolt played a major role in its collapse.

**Dates BCE**

| | |
|---|---|
| c. 3000 | Sumerian city-states begin growing; writing is invented in Mesopotamia. |
| 2360–2180 | Period of Akkadian rule over Mesopotamia. |
| c. 1800–c.1600 | Babylon dominates Mesopotamia; Hammurabi produces the first written laws in Western history. |
| c. 1600–c. 1200 | The kingdoms of Mitanni and the Kassites rise and fall. |
| c. 900 | Assyria enters its period of greatest territorial expansion. |
| 720 | The kingdom of Israel falls to the Assyrian king Sargon II. |
| 701 | The Assyrians lay siege to the city of Jerusalem but fail to take it. Judah remains independent, although it must pay tribute to Assyria. |
| 612 | A coalition of Medes, Chaldeans, and Persians overthrows Assyria. The capital city of Nineveh is destroyed. |
| 586 | The Chaldean Babylonians, led by Nebuchadnezzar, capture Jerusalem; the Babylonian Exile of the Jews begins. It will last until 539 BCE. |
| 550 | Achaemenid Persia, under Cyrus the Great, begins its conquest of Mesopotamia. |
| 539 | Persia conquers Babylon. |
| 525 | Egypt falls to the Persians. |
| 490 | Persia fails in its attempt to invade Greece when it is defeated at the battle of Marathon. A second attempt ten years later also ends in defeat. |
| 330 | Alexander the Great captures Persepolis and brings down Achaemenid Persia. |
| 323 | Alexander the Great dies; his empire is divided among his generals. Ptolemy is given Egypt, while Seleucus takes control of Persia. |
| c. 250 | Parthia begins its expansion. |
| 64 | Rome erases what little remains of the Seleucid Empire; thirty-three years later, it turns Ptolemaic Egypt into a Roman province. A period of intense warfare with Parthia begins. |

**Dates CE**

| | |
|---|---|
| 117 | Rome briefly occupies Parthian Mesopotamia. |
| c. 200 | Sassanid Persia replaces Parthia as the Middle East's imperial power. |

| | |
|---|---|
| 395 | The Roman Empire is split in half. The Eastern Empire makes its capital at Constantinople and becomes known as the Byzantine Empire. The Byzantines and Sassanids start fighting. |
| 476 | The Western Roman Empire collapses. |
| 570 | The Prophet Muhammad is born in the Arabian city of Mecca. |
| 610–632 | The religion of Islam grows and comes to dominate the Arabian Peninsula. After the capture of Mecca, Muhammad dies in 632. |
| 632–1000 | An Islamic empire is established in the Middle East and North Africa. Islam threatens the Byzantine world and takes root in Spain. |
| 1095–1274 | European Christian Crusaders invade the Middle East and try to conquer it. They ultimately fail, and Islam reigns supreme throughout the region. |
| 1258 | Mongol armies reach Baghdad and destroy it. A Mongol empire that rules South Asia, Iran, and Mesopotamia is established. |
| 1300 | The Ottoman Turks establish an empire of their own after the Mongols retreat from Turkish territory. |
| 1453 | An Ottoman army captures Constantinople, renaming it Istanbul, and wipes out what remains of the Byzantine Empire. |
| c. 1500–c. 1900 | Ottoman Turkey rules over a vast Middle Eastern empire and fights repeated wars against Christian Europe. |
| 1914 | World War I begins; Turkey sides with Germany and Austria-Hungary. |
| 1916 | The great Arab revolt against the Ottomans begins. |
| 1918 | Turkey surrenders to the Western Allies, ending World War I and Ottoman rule in the Middle East. A democratic republic of Turkey replaces the empire. |
| 2003 | The United States invades Iraq, two years after doing likewise in Afghanistan. The U.S. sets its goal as the creation of a peaceful, democratic Middle East. America thus becomes the latest power to try to unite the region under its leadership. |
| 2006 | Iran and the United States enter into a contest for regional influence. Once again, as in the days of Alexander and Darius, the West and what was Persia come into conflict. |

## Chapter 1. The Plain of Gaugamela, 331 BCE

1. Thomas Cahill, *Sailing the Wine Dark Sea: Why the Greeks Matter* (New York: Doubleday, 2003), p. 168.

2. J.F.C. Fuller, *A Military History of the Western World: Volume I, From the Earliest Times to the Battle of Lepanto* (New York: De Capo, 1954), p. 100.

3. Ibid., p. 104.

4. Michael Grant, *The Founders of the Western World: A History of Greece and Rome* (New York: Barnes and Noble, 1991), p. 115.

## Chapter 2. Mesopotamia of Old

1. C. Leonard Woolley, *The Sumerians* (New York: W.W. Norton and Company, 1965), p. 13.

2. Jorgen Laessoe, *People of Assyria*, translated by F.S. Leigh-Browne (New York: Barnes and Noble, Inc., 1963), p. 24.

3. "Hammurabi's Code of Law," translated by L.W. King. http://eawc.evansville.edu/anthology/hammurabi.htm

4. David Ferry, *Gilgamesh: A New Rendering in English Verse* (New York: The Noonday Press, 1993), p. 4.

## Chapter 3. Mighty Assyria

1. Robert William Rogers, *A History of Babylonia and Assyria, Volume I* (New York: Eaton and Maine, 1900; reprint, Long Beach, California: Lost Arts Media, 2003), p. 308.

2. Oliver Lyman Spaulding and Hoffman Nickerson, *Ancient and Medieval Warfare* (New York: Barnes and Noble Books, 1993), p. 20.

3. A.T. Olmstead, *History of Assyria* (Chicago: University of Chicago Press, 1951), p. 645.

4. Holy Bible, King James Version, 2 Kings 17:21, 23.

5. Ibid., 19:33–34.

6. Ibid., 19:35–36.

## Chapter 4. Chaldeans and Achaemenids

1. Jorgen Laessoe, *People of Assyria*, translated by F.S. Leigh-Browne (New York: Barnes and Noble, Inc., 1963), p. 105.

2. Tom Holland, *Persian Fire: The First World Empire and the Battle for the West* (New York: Doubleday, 2005), p. 6.

3. Robert William Rogers, *A History of Babylonia and Assyria, Volume I* (New York: Eaton and Maine, 1900; reprint, Long Beach, California: Lost Arts Media, 2003), p. 280.

4. Holy Bible, King James Version, 2 Kings 25:21.

5. William Culican, *The Medes and the Persians* (New York: Frederick A. Praeger, 1965), p. 170.

6. Holland, p. xviii.

7. Holy Bible, Isaiah 44:6.

## Chapter 5. Alexander's Empire and Beyond

1. Tom Holland, *Persian Fire: The First World Empire and the Battle for the West* (New York: Doubleday, 2005), p. 361.

2. Oliver Lyman Spaulding and Hoffman Nickerson, *Ancient and Medieval Warfare* (New York: Barnes and Noble Books, 1993), p. 86.

3. A.B. Bosworth, *Conquest and Empire: The Reign of Alexander the Great* (New York: Cambridge University Press, 1988), p. 175.

## Chapter 6. The Borderland of Empire

1. Tom Holland, *Rubicon: The Last Years of the Roman Republic* (New York: Doubleday, 2003), p. 259.

2. Antonio Santosuosso, *Storming the Heavens: Soldiers, Emperors, and Civilians in the Roman Empire* (Boulder, Colorado: Westview Press, 2001), p. 117.

3. Ibid.

## Chapter 7. East vs. West

1. Elton L. Daniel, *The History of Iran* (Westport, Connecticut: Greenwood Press, 2001), p. 57.

2. Oliver Lyman Spaulding and Hoffman Nickerson, *Ancient and Medieval Warfare* (New York: Barnes and Noble Books, 1993), p. 267.

## Chapter 8. Holy Warriors—An Islamic Middle East

1. Karen Armstrong, *Muhammad: A Biography of the Prophet* (San Francisco: HarperSanFrancisco, 1992), p. 45.

2. Allama Sir Abdullah Al-Mamun Al-Suhrawardy, editors, *The Wisdom of Muhammad* (New York: Citadel Press, 2001), p. 46.

3. Arthur Goldschmidt, Jr., *A Concise History of the Middle East* (Boulder, Colorado: Westview Books, 2002), p. 40.

4. Ibid., p. 60.

5. James Reston Jr., *Warriors of God: Richard the Lionheart and Saladin in the Third Crusade* (New York: Doubleday, 2001), p. 319.

## Chapter 9. Allah's Empire—The Ottoman Turks

1. David Willis McCullogh, editor, *Chronicles of the Barbarians: Firsthand Accounts of Pillage and Conquest, From the Ancient World to the Fall of Constantinople* (New York: History Book Club, 1998), p. 318.

2. Ibid., p. 315.

3. Ibid., p. 367.

## Books

Barter, James. *The Ancient Persians*. San Diego: Lucent Books, 2005.

Greenblatt, Miriam. *Suleyman the Magnificent and the Ottoman Empire*. New York: Benchmark Books, 2003.

Nardo, Don. *The Assyrian Empire*. San Diego: Lucent Books, 2005.

Podany, Amanda H. *The Ancient Near Eastern World*. New York: Oxford University Press, 2005.

Reece, Katherine. *The Persians: Warriors of the Ancient World*. Vero Beach, Florida: Rourke Publishing, 2005.

Ruggiero, Adriane. *The Ottoman Empire*. New York: Benchmark Books, 2003.

Saggs, H.W.F. *Everyday Life in Babylonia and Assyria*. New York: Dorset Books, 1987.

Shuter, Jane. *Mesopotamia*. Chicago: Heinemann Library, 2006.

Stefoff, Rebecca. *The Ancient Near East*. New York: Benchmark Books, 2005.

## Works Consulted

Al-Mamun Al-Suhrawardy, Allama Sir Abdullah, editors. *The Wisdom of Muhammad*. New York: Citadel Press, 2001.

Armstrong, Karen. *Muhammad: A Biography of the Prophet*. San Francisco: HarperSanFrancisco, 1992.

Bosworth, A.B. *Conquest and Empire: The Reign of Alexander the Great*. New York: Cambridge University Press, 1988.

Cahill, Thomas. *Sailing the Wine Dark Sea: Why the Greeks Matter*. New York: Doubleday, 2003.

Culican, William. *The Medes and the Persians*. New York: Frederick A. Praeger, 1965.

Daniel, Elton L. *The History of Iran*. Westport, Connecticut: Greenwood Press, 2001.

Fuller, J.F.C. *A Military History of the Western World: Volume I, From the Earliest Times to the Battle of Lepanto*. New York: De Capo, 1954.

Goldschmidt, Arthur, Jr. *A Concise History of the Middle East*. Boulder, Colorado: Westview Books, 2002.

Grant, Michael. *The Founders of the Western World: A History of Greece and Rome*. New York: Barnes and Noble, 1991.

Holland, Tom. *Persian Fire: The First World Empire and the Battle for the West*. New York: Doubleday, 2005.

———. *Rubicon: The Last Years of the Roman Republic* (New York: Doubleday, 2003.

Laessoe, Jorgen. *People of Assyria*. Translated by F.S. Leigh-Browne. New York: Barnes and Noble, Inc., 1963.

McCullough, David Willis, editor. *Chronicles of the Barbarians: Firsthand Accounts of Pillage and Conquest, From the Ancient World to the Fall of Constantinople*. New York: History Book Club, 1998.

Olmstead, A.T. *History of Assyria*. Chicago: University of Chicago Press, 1951.

Rogers, Robert William. *A History of Babylonia and Assyria, Volume I*. New York: Eaton and Maine, 1900; reprint, Long Beach, California: Lost Arts Media, 2003.

Santosuosso, Antonio. *Storming the Heavens: Soldiers, Emperors, and Civilians in the Roman Empire*. Boulder, Colorado: Westview Press, 2001.

Spaulding, Oliver Lyman, and Hoffman Nickerson. *Ancient and Medieval Warfare*. New York: Barnes and Noble Books, 1993.

Woolley, C. Leonard. *The Sumerians*. New York: W.W. Norton and Company, 1965.

## On the Internet

Ancient Civilizations
http://www.princetonol.com/groups/iad/lessons/middle/ancient.htm

Cybersleuth Kids, Ancient Civilizations
http://cybersleuth-kids.com/sleuth/
History/Ancient_Civilizations/Ancient_
Middle_East/index.htm

Egypt and the Ancient Near East Web
Resources for Young People and Teachers
http://oi.uchicago.edu/OI/DEPT/RA/
ABZU/YOUTH_RESOURCES.HTML

Hammurabi's Code of Law, trans. L.W. King.
http://eawc.evansville.edu/anthology/
hammurabi.htm

History in the News: The Middle East http://
www.albany.edu/history/middle-east/

Islam and Islamic History in Arabia and the
Middle East
http://www.islamicity.com/Mosque/
ihame/Sec13.htm

Mesopotamia
http://www.wsu.edu/~dee/MESO/
MESO.HTM

Middle Eastern History
http://www.tntech.edu/history/
mideast.html

The Ottomans
http://www.theottomans.org/english/
history/index.asp

Social Studies for Kids, The Ancient Middle
East
http://www.socialstudiesforkids.com/
subjects/ancientmiddleeast.htm

Time for Kids
http://www.timeforkids.com/TFK/class/
reproducibles/theme/
0,17836,Middle~East,00.html

# Glossary

**autonomous** (aw-TAH-nuh-mus)—Able to self-govern.

**caliph** (KAA-lif)—A civil and spiritual leader of Islam after Muhammad.

**cataphract** (KAA-tah-frakt)—A cavalryman who, with his horse, wore full body armor

**Crusader** (kroo-SAY-der)—A Christian soldier of the eleventh, twelfth, or thirteenth century who fought to win the Holy Land from the Muslims.

**cuneiform** (kyoo-NEE-ih-form)—Wedge-shaped writing.

**diorite** (DY-uh-ryt)—A granular igneous rock.

**imperial** (im-PIR-ee-ul)—Having to do with an emperor or empire.

**janissary** (JAH-nih-say-ree)—One of an elite group of Turkish soldiers.

**mercenary** (MER-suh-nayr-ee)—A soldier who is paid to fight by a country other than his own.

**monolatry** (muh-NAH-luh-tree)—Worshiping one god in a group of many.

**monotheism** (mah-moh-THEE-izm)—Belief in only one god.

**polytheism** (PAH-lee-thee-izm)—Belief in more than one god.

**satrap** (SAY-trap)—A governor in ancient Persia. The governed area was called a satrapy (SAY-traa-pee).

**stela** (STEE-luh)—A carved stone slab or pillar.

**triumvirate** (try-UM-vuh-rit)—A group or association of three.

# Index

# About the Author

John Davenport holds a Ph.D. in History from the University of Connecticut and is the author of numerous books on subjects ranging from biography to historical geography. His published works include a history of the Nuremburg war crimes trials and a biography of the medieval Muslim leader Saladin. Davenport teaches social studies at Corte Madera Middle School in Portola Valley, California. He lives in San Carlos, California, with his wife, Jennifer, and his two sons, William and Andrew.